FITNESS WALKING

Other books by James Rippe, M.D.

Manual of Cardiovascular Diagnosis and Management
Manual of Intensive Care Medicine
Intensive Care Medicine

Other books by Frank Katch, Ed.D.

Nutrition, Weight Control, and Exercise
Getting in Shape
Exercise Physiology: Food, Energy and Human Performance

FITNESS WALKING

Robert Sweetgall,
James Rippe, M.D.,
and Frank Katch, Ed.D.

with John Dignam

Illustrations by Frederick Bush

A Perigee Book

Perigee Books
are published by
The Putnam Publishing Group
200 Madison Avenue
New York, NY 10016

Published simultaneously in Canada by
General Publishing Co. Limited, Toronto

Library of Congress Cataloging in Publication Data

Sweetgall, Robert.
  Fitness walking.

  1. Walking.   2. Physical fitness.   I. Rippe,
James M.   II. Katch, Frank I.   III. Title.
GV199.5.S977   1985   613.7′1   85-9572
ISBN 0-399-51149-0

Book design by ARLENE SCHLEIFER GOLDBERG

Printed in the United States of America
                9   10

To my best teachers: my parents, Sylvia and Murray,
and Dr. Robert E. Neeves.

And to the hundreds of kind and trusting Americans
who refueled my body and spirit
in times of need along the way.

Seven hundred miles into his 50-state walk, Rob leads two marching bands in celebrating the fiftieth anniversary of Toledo's Pearson Metropark. Photo by John Lusk, "Citizens for Metropark."

OR THE HEALTH OF IT

84   9   30

ACKNOWLEDGMENTS

Our heartfelt thanks to our many colleagues and friends who helped and supported us in this effort: to Carol L. Cone, whose genius brought us together and whose vision sustained us; to Bruce Katz of The Rockport Company and Bill Gore, Peter Gilson and the associates of Gore-Tex Fabrics, thanks for ongoing support and encouragement throughout the walk; to Kerry, David, Kevin, Ellen, Roma, Guin and Bill; Dr. Joseph Dautlick and the DuPont Biomedical Products Department; Bill Spiker and the artists of Lyons Studios; Harry Nelson; Florence Cantarera of the Retired Senior Volunteers Program; Paul Gerritson; Ginny and Al Brown; Linda Patton; Bill Martin; Fred Dingle; Bill Murray; the Floyd Hudson State Service Center; to Dr. Jessica Ross and Marion Gurry who admirably performed the physiologic testing on Rob at the U. Mass. Medical School; to Dr. Kevin Campbell, Dr. Patty Freedson, Dr. Bob Andreas and Dr. William Byrnes in the Exercise Science Department at U. Mass., Amherst, and Dr. Ken Samonds and Maxine Brenner in the Food, Science and Nutrition Department at U. Mass., Amherst, and their students for conducting the studies on biomechanics, exercise psyiology and dietary intake; to Dr. Jon Kabat-Zinn, who developed the pointers on flexibility and mental strategies; to the enthusiastic staff of Cone & Company, particularly Lynn Rubenson, Mark Shea, Roy Anderson and Jon Zemmol, who made sure the task went smoothly; and to Dr. William Rossi, who offered helpful comments and advice on foot care and shoes.

Finally to Adrienne Ingrum, our editor, who pushed us when necessary, consoled us when we felt discouraged and did a super job of pulling the project together.

CONTENTS

PREFACE   13

INTRODUCTION   23

1. WHY WALK?   43

Health Benefits of Walking • Safety Advantages of Walking • The Myth of "No Pain, No Gain"

2. A CARDIOLOGIST'S VIEW OF WALKING   51

Walking and Health • What Is Fitness Walking? • Special
Medical Aspects of Walking • Testing Rob Sweetgall • The Ex-
ercise Tolerance Test • Running • Lifetime Exercise versus
Short-Term Conditioning

3. THE FITNESS PROGRAM FOR EVERYONE: HOW TO
RATE YOUR WALKING FITNESS   64

Step 1: How to Take Your Pulse • Step 2: The Step Test for Men
and Women • Step 3: How to Interpret Your Score

4. GETTING READY FOR FITNESS WALKING   73

Mental Benefits of Walking • Shoes • Foot Care • Walking
Tips • Exercises for Flexibility • Strength • Motor Control

5. YOUR FITNESS WALKING PROGRAM FROM STARTER
TO EXPERT   111

Safety: The Preprogram Evaluation • Learning Your Target Heart
Rate • The Programs: Starter, Beginner, Intermediate, Advanced, Expert • Maintenance Programs

6. **FOOD FOR THE ROAD**   129

What Is the Best Diet? • Nutrition Throughout Life • Nutrition Tips for Fitness Walkers • Nutrition and the Energy Value of Foods

7. **FITNESS WALKING FOR CARDIAC REHABILITATION**   145

The Scope of the Problem • Comprehensive Cardiac Rehabilitation • Phases of Cardiac Rehabilitation • Fitness Walking Principles for Cardiac Rehabilitation • Protocols for Cardiac Rehabilitation

8. **WALKING AND TOTAL FITNESS**   155

GREAT WALKING PERFORMANCES   163

FITNESS WALKING DAILY LOG   164

FITNESS WALKING

Layering up for warmth during 300-mile stretch of walking on crushed ice and snow from central Montana to Stevens Pass, Washington. Temperatures ranged from −10 to 20 degrees.

PREFACE

I am a walker. Walking is my hobby, exercise, medicine and profession. It is my life.

I tour, visit schools and interested communities, conduct walking fitness clinics and interview with the news media, all to spread the word about our safest, easiest, most beneficial exercise—walking. Using America's highways as my stage, I walk in the hope that people will be moved by my example to walk for their health.

On September 7, 1984, I began a fifty-state, 11,600-mile "Walk for the Health of It." Carrying just a five-pound waist pack, I traveled light and lived simply—walking, talking, eating and sleeping. At schools and civic clubs and town squares, I talked about walking.

I was not always like this. For many years, fitness and health were not big factors in my life. In 1976, my father, an aunt and two uncles died of heart disease. In 1981, motivated by this family history, I left a well-paying twelve-year chemical engineering career to initiate a 10,600-mile trek along the perimeter of the United States, and 279 days later, I had jogged and walked my way through 37 states and three western blizzards. I had talked to 100,000 students on fitness and heart disease, worn out 25 pairs of shoes and pounded on 80 blisters—all in the name of health.

As an exercise fitness "salesman," I'll admit to having failures as well as successes. The successes stand out. A sixth grader wrote, "Rob, if you can do 10,000 miles around the country, I think I can walk a couple of miles for exercise." A Delaware physical education teacher kicked the cigarette

habit after my school assembly, and a high school boy came up to me and asked, "If I stop smoking now, what can I expect?" These successes fueled the spirit. If only one percent of my audience for that first trek acted on the message, that was 1000 people who were giving health—and themselves—a better chance.

On July 15, 1983, that perimeter tour ended, and a weatherworn, tired, journeyman walker sank deep into his corduroy couch to debate the future. Should I return to my chemical engineering career? That was easy street—money, security, a nest egg, insurance. A road often taken. But I took the less traveled path, as poet Robert Frost would have described it: out on the highway.

On a spring night in 1984, under the white cone of my desk lamp, I started dreaming. State road maps were sprawled out and magic markers squeaked along a new route, village by village, town by town. This time, fifty states, one year, all walking. Running, the exercise that had cost me 80 blisters and unnecessary leg soreness and foot pain on my first trip, would not be part of this new journey.

I contacted several school administrators and news reporters who had participated in my first trek and asked if they would be interested again. "Sure, why not," came the response.

Still, I needed support, the kind that buys food and lodging. Two weeks later, Peter Gilson of Gore-Tex Fabrics listened, questioned and nodded approval with a smile.

A month later, I sat in a dim Boston restaurant, crunching on string beans and broccoli across a big, round pine table from Bruce Katz, president of the Rockport Company. Between bites, the young walking-shoe company executive listened to my plan. By dessert came his answer: "Yes." I was set with financial backing for the long haul. Also at the table was Dr. James Rippe, a cardiologist at the University of Massachusetts Medical School, who soon organized a team of colleagues to scientifically research and document the physical effects of the walk.

Now it is February 12, 1985, and the journey is 5000 miles old, almost half done. Last spring's dreams of sparkling blue highways are now a reality of sun-baked, cracked asphalt. Here in the timeless Mojave, I

◀ *Rob is greeted by teacher Greg Peck and a gathering of 100 students on his walk through the Bavarian Village of Leavenworth, Washington. Day 106, 3200-mile mark.* Photo by Nadra Rivers.

15

The elementary school students of Waterville, Washington, watch Rob intently as he demonstrates the hip flexor/extensor static stretches for them. Photo by Nadra Rivers.

◀ *Regardless of weather conditions, Rob stops to perform essential foot care with assorted balms and lotions. Day 106.*

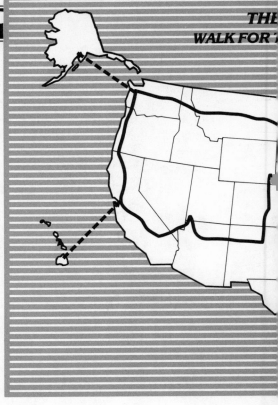

THE JOURNEY

On September 7, 1984, Rob Sweetgall began walking WEST. Leaving his home town of Newark, Delaware, carrying only a light waist pack, Rob plans to reach Chicago via Michigan in 33 days, traverse Montana and the Continental Divide in early December, and climb the Cascades' Wall of Evergreens to reach Seattle by Christmas. A SOUTHERN course along the misting Pacific (January, 1985) to San Francisco will follow. Five thousand miles into the journey, Rob will turn EAST to cross the Mojave and Painted Deserts and Rockies. From the Central Plains, Rob will sweep through Louisiana's bayous to New Orleans and onto Mobile before heading NORTH on the spine of the Appalachian Mountains to Washington, D.C. The 'last leg' includes a walk along the Hudson and a loop of New England with a final descent on Manhattan. Including shuttles to Alaska and Hawaii, the trek totals 11,600 miles on foot and all 50 states. One year of traveling light.

THE START

Sep	7	Newark	DE	1
Sep	7	Elkton	MD	2
Sep	10	Westminster	MD	
Sep	11	Hagerstown	MD	
Sep	14	Cumberland	MD	
Sep	17	Uniontown	PA	3
Sep	18	Wheeling	WV	4
Sep	20	Cambridge	OH	5
Sep	21	Zanesville	OH	
Sep	23	Columbus	OH	
Sep	27	Findlay	OH	

WALKING THE ERIE CANAL TOWPATH TO THE CITY OF METROPARKS, TOLEDO

Sep	29	Toledo	OH	
Oct	1	Detroit	MI	6
Oct	4	Flint/Owosso	MI	
Oct	5	Lansing	MI	
Oct	6	Battle Creek	MI	
Oct	7	Kalamazoo	MI	
Oct	9	South Bend	IN	7

FROM FARM FIELDS TO INDUSTRIAL STACKS TO LAKE SHORE DRIVE

Oct	10	Chicago	IL	8
Oct	14	Waukegan	IL	
Oct	15	Milwaukee	WI	9
Oct	18	Madison	WI	

CROSSING THE MISSISSIPPI AND ALONG HER ROLLING BLUFFS

Oct	20	Dubuque	IA	10
Oct	23	Guttenburg	IA	
Oct	24	Decorah	IA	
Oct	27	Rochester	MN	11
Oct	29	Twin Cities	MN	
Nov	2	Willmar	MN	
Nov	5	Milbank	SD	12
Nov	8	Aberdeen	SD	
Nov	11	Mobridge	SD	
Nov	14	Lemmon	SD	
Nov	15	Hettinger	ND	13
Nov	16	Bowman	ND	
Nov	18	Baker	MT	14

OIL CATTLE & TWO PEOPLE PER SQUARE MILE

Nov	20	Miles City	MT	
Nov	25	Billings	MT	
Nov	30	Big Timber	MT	
Dec	2	Bozeman Pass	MT	
Dec	3	Three Forks	MT	
Dec	5	Helena	MT	

THE CONTINENTAL DIVIDE AT McDONALD'S PASS ELEV. 6330 FT.

Dec	9	Missoula	MT	
Dec	12	Lookout Pass	ID	15

FROM MOUNTAIN TO PACIFIC TIME: INTO IDAHO'S SILVER HILLS

Dec	13	Couer'd Alene	ID	
Dec	14	Spokane	WA	16
Dec	18	Coulee City	WA	
Dec	20	Wenatchee	WA	

CLIMBING THE CASCADES VIA STEVENS PASS ONTO PUGET SOUND

Dec	25	Seattle	WA	
Dec	27	Tacoma	WA	
Dec	30	Anchorage	AK	17
Jan	1	Olympia	WA	

IN THE DUST SHADOW OF MOUNT SAINT HELENS

Jan	3	Portland	OR	18
Jan	6	Salem	OR	
Jan	7	Corvallis	OR	
Jan	8	Eugene	OR	
Jan	11	Roseburg	OR	
Jan	13	Grants Pass	OR	
Jan	14	Medford	OR	
Jan	16	Yreka	CA	19

MT. SHASTA — 14,600 FEET TALL LOOKING OVER SACRAMENTO'S VALLEY

Jan	19	Redding	CA	
Jan	24	Sacramento	CA	
Jan	27	San Francisco	CA	

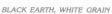

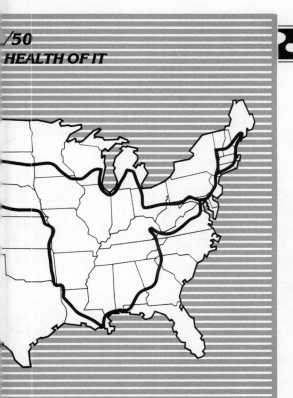

A ONE DAY SHUTTLE TO
HAWAII

Jan	28	Honolulu	HI	20
Jan	31	San Jose	CA	
Feb	5	Fresno	CA	
Feb	9	Bakersfield	CA	

BIG TREES...DRY LAKES:
SEQUOIA NAT'L FORREST...
MOJAVE DESERT

Feb	10	Mojave	CA	
Feb	13	Barstow	CA	
Feb	14	Baker	CA	
Feb	17	Las Vegas	NV	21
Feb	22	Mesquite	NV	
Feb	26	Mt. Carmel	UT	22
Mar	1	Page	AZ	23
Mar	3	Tuba City	AZ	
Mar	6	Flagstaff	AZ	

THE HALFWAY POINT OF THE
JOURNEY: WHITE SNOW AND
MAGENTA SANDS — THE
GRAND CANYON & PAINTED
DESERT

Mar	12	Gallup	NM	24
Mar	18	Albuquerque	NM	
Mar	20	Santa Fe	NM	
Mar	23	Taos	NM	
Mar	26	Trinidad	CO	25
Mar	29	Pueblo	CO	
Mar	30	Col Springs	CO	

NORTH ON THE MILE-HIGH
PLATEAU: ROCKIES TO THE
WEST, KANSAS WHEAT FIELDS
TO THE EAST

Apr	2	Denver	CO	
Apr	6	Greely	CO	
Apr	8	Cheyenne	WY	26
Apr	15	North Platte	NE	27
Apr	21	Grand Island	NE	

BLACK EARTH, WHITE GRAIN
ELEVATORS

Apr	23	Lincoln	NE	
Apr	29	Topeka	KS	28
May	1	Kansas City	MO	29
May	5	Chanute	KS	
May	9	Tulsa	OK	30
May	19	Paris	TX	31
May	21	Texarkana	AR	32
May	24	Shreveport	LA	33
May	29	Alexandria	LA	

RIVERS, BAYOUS & SWAMPS
PLUS ATCHAFALAYA'S
FLOODWAY

Jun	1	Baton Rouge	LA	
Jun	4	New Orleans	LA	
Jun	9	Gulfport	MS	34

WALKING THE SEA WALL ON
THE OLD SPANISH TRAIL BY
THE GULF BEACHES

Jun	11	Mobile	AL	35
Jun	14	Century	FL	36
Jun	15	Brewton	AL	
Jun	18	Montgomery	AL	
Jun	20	Alexander City	AL	

FIRST DAY OF SUMMER ON
THE GEORGIA PLAINS

Jun	23	Newnam	GA	37
Jun	24	Atlanta	GA	
Jun	26	Gainesville	GA	
Jun	29	Greenville	SC	38
Jul	1	Ashville	NC	39

APPALACHIAN SHADE & BLUE
RIDGE BEAUTY

Jul	4	Johnson City	TN	40
Jul	4	Kingsport	TN	
Jul	6	Big Stone Gap	VA	41
Jul	7	Jenkins	KY	42
Jul	10	Bluefield	VA	
Jul	12	Blacksburg	VA	
Jul	15	Lynchburg	VA	
Jul	17	Charlottesville	VA	
Jul	22	Alexandria	VA	

10,000 MILES INTO THE
JOURNEY

Jul	22	Washington	DC	
Jul	23	College Park	MD	
Jul	24	Baltimore	MD	
Jul	26	Elkton	MD	
Jul	26	Newark	DE	
Jul	27	Wilmington	DE	
Jul	29	Philadelphia	PA	

CROSSING THE DELAWARE
ON OLD BEN FRANKLIN

Jul	30	Cherry Hill	NJ	43
Jul	31	Trenton	NJ	
Aug	2	Newark/Wayne	NJ	
Aug	3	Spring Valley	NY	44
Aug	5	West Point	NY	

FOLLOWING THE HUDSON,
NORTH

Aug	5	Newburgh	NY	
Aug	6	Kingston	NY	
Aug	8	Albany	NY	
Aug	10	Bennington	VT	45

THE GREEN MOUNTAINS:
MAPLES & SYRUP

Aug	11	Brattleboro	VT	
Aug	11	Keene	NH	46
Aug	13	Manchester	NH	
Aug	14	Concord	NH	
Aug	15	Dover	NH	
Aug	17	Portland	ME	47

MAINE'S COAST: WHITE FOAM
ON GRANITE ROCKS & SANDY
BEACHES

Aug	19	Portsmouth	NH	
Aug	19	Hampton Bch.	NH	
Aug	20	Boston	MA	48
Aug	23	Plymouth	MA	

AT THE ROCK ACROSS FROM
THE CAPE

Aug	23	New Bedford	MA	
Aug	25	Fall River	MA	
Aug	26	Newport	RI	49
Aug	27	Warwick	RI	
Aug	28	Providence	RI	
Aug	29	Marlboro	MA	
Aug	30	Worcester	MA	
Aug	30	Springfield	MA	

APPROACHING THE 50TH
STATE OF THE TREK AT
ENFIELD, CONNECTICUT

Aug	31	Hartford	CN	50
Sep	2	New Haven	CN	
Sep	3	Bridgeport	CN	
Sep	3	Stamford	CN	
Sep	4	Greenwich	CN	
Sep	4	White Plains	NY	

A MARATON WALK FROM
THE FINISH

| Sep | 5 | Mount Vernon | NY | |
| Sep | 5 | Manhattan | NY | |

THE FINISH

search the sagebrush and the Joshua trees for precious shade away from where the rattlers sleep. Occasional desert shacks, protected by tall barbed-wire fences and growling dogs, remind me that I am on my own. To dissolve loneliness, I recall great times of the past—the 150 fifth graders who walked with me the opening three and a half miles; the two North Dakota ranchers who walked for three days and 101 miles with me. Just recently I met a San Raphael lady on her mile walk to the Saturday night movies. She passed the theater for seven miles of exercise and company through Sausalito. Five days later a bus driver named Mike recognized my face in Palo Alto and spontaneously tagged along, saying, "Ever since my last junker broke down, I've been walking to work—two miles each day and twice that on double-shift days. I've lost twenty-five pounds over the past year." Mike went on to discuss a young lady he met at the 1985 Super Bowl. "I'd like to take her out . . . but the awkwardness of it all. You know with no wheels . . ." "How about a walking dinner date? You'll probably get to know her better," I suggested. Mike nodded in agreement.

We have a choice—to stay within our shells or to crawl out. In Santa Barbara, a man who saw me approaching his patch of sidewalk darted back from his mailbox to lock his front-yard black iron gates with fumbling tension in his fingers. Oh, what we keep inside us . . . I bring all this up because I feel that there is more to walking than pure fitness. Sure, aerobic conditioning is important, as is weight and blood pressure control, diet and stress. As you read on, you'll find out how important. But there is something else captured within these pages—positive attitude and the will to do. For you, as well as I, can open fence doors and walk across America in your own special way. Then we can all discover who our neighbors are.

Rob Sweetgall
crossing the Mojave Desert
Day 159 (near Victorville, California)

◀ *Sweetgall and Bruce Katz, president of The Rockport Company, discuss the future of walking in America while climbing McDonald's Pass at the Continental Divide, west of Helena, Montana. Photo by Fred Smith Associates.*

INTRODUCTION: A WALK FOR ALL AMERICA

Dorlene was a meticulous woman. It showed in her peanut butter and honey sandwiches, the best triple deckers I had ever tasted. It wasn't so much the ingredients as the preparation, the way she evenly trowled each fresh slice of whole-wheat bread with the care of a skilled mason working on a class-one concrete finish. Just the right proportions. The morning air would do the rest, congealing the honey into a thin, sweet sheet of ice that cracked upon biting to fool my tongue into believing that "smooth" was "crunchy." I wanted her to take her time in preparing them because I knew the wind would be waiting for me once I stepped outside the house in Worden, Montana, where she and her husband Ken Boulten had put me up. Almost three months earlier I had stepped out to the warmth of summer and a crowd of people on a Delaware street as I started an 11,600-mile walk through America.

That morning I could hear the wind cheering outside on the empty

◀ *Seventy students from Helena Middle School and Anderson Junior High School join Rob for the climb to the top of McDonald's Pass on December 5, 1984.* Photo by Fred Smith Associates.

road. The same wind that had assaulted me in Litchfield, Minnesota, and in the Dakotas, pulling tears from my eyes and freezing them on my cheeks like candle wax. That morning I was thousands of miles from home with thousands of miles to go. Ahead were miles of fields, no known stops, uncertain weather and hours alone. There was nothing to do but walk.

I stepped into the cold predawn morning and reminded myself that I had "promises to keep." I was engaged in a "Walk for All America," to dramatize the message of health and fitness. My slogan is "Walk for the Health of It," but traveling America at four miles an hour yields, a lot more than good health.

As I reflected on two years, two trips, 22,000 miles, 36 million steps, 50 states, three million burned calories and 30 pairs of shoes, I chuckled at the thought that it had all started with a quarter-mile jog on a country road in Delaware. It had started because I looked in the mirror and didn't like the shape of things. I was about 30 pounds overweight, and years of being "normally inactive," as so many of us are, had robbed my muscles of tone. Coupled with fear of heart disease, which ran in my family, I warned myself to become physically fit. In the twelve years since that 1970 jog, I had run myself into shape, quit my job as a chemical engineer, founded a public charity called the Foundation for the Development of Cardiovascular Health and was now on my second walking trip around the country.

As my feet settled into the rhythm of the day, I wondered how the kid who spent the first twenty-one years of his life in Brooklyn, got from sewer stickball to Montana sagebrush, from subways to prairie sunsets. Quite simply, I walked. One thing that arouses new parents' cheers is their baby's first step. Learning to walk brings out the cameras and applause, but walking soon takes second place to bicycles and automobiles.

My first big walk was a six-mile hike on a country road in the New York Catskills, a walk around the world, it seemed. My Uncle Joe, cousin Sidney and I, age seven, set off after Saturday morning breakfast. Three miles and two hours later Sidney and I had our thumbs out for a hitch home. We went halfway around the world, I guess.

I was never really an athlete. The high school bookworm, the scholar, good at math and science, I played some basketball, a little bit of racquet sports, and varsity bowling in high school and college. To qualify for the two-credit freshman physical education course in college we had to run one mile. I practiced, ran a 6:09 mile and became sick. But I had accomplished something.

Needless to say, I was never an elite athlete. No speed, nothing to make me varsity material for the big sports. I was always a little bit overweight, five or ten pounds, and I found myself gaining weight in college. In 1965, when I was a college freshman at Cooper Union, the blackout struck New York City and Sweetgall the long-distance walker surfaced again. I was bringing my bowling ball home that night on the subway, along with my stuffed attaché case. The train stopped dead and I came up to the darkness of Fulton Street and a New York City I could not see. Some people partied and some stayed put, but I sensed a challenge. I walked with my sixteen-pound bowling ball and attaché case over the Brooklyn Bridge, home. The walk was seven miles.

Unfortunately, there are some things we have to learn through experience. I have yet to meet a family in America whose history is free of heart disease. My family was no different. In 1970, when I looked in the mirror and didn't like what I saw, my father was having problems with his heart. I began thinking about health as I jogged a quarter of a mile at a time, then a half mile. After a few months I tried a three-mile run. The body has a nice feeling to it when it moves, and I liked the feeling, the accomplishment. Fractions of miles became three and four miles a day.

Dr. Robert Neeves of the University of Delaware, an exercise physiologist and a man to whom I owe a great deal for getting me on the road to fitness, gave an inspirational talk at a DuPont meeting on safety. He spoke on risk factors in heart disease. It confirmed that the exercise I was getting was good for me. Dr. Neeves was the role model for what I am doing today.

In 1976, my father died of heart disease and soon after, on three consecutive weekends, an aunt and two uncles also died of heart disease. When you see the penalties one pays for not taking care of health in your own family, when you go to the hospital and watch it happen between those blank, white walls, it leaves a powerful impression.

There were other problems in the family as well—high blood pressure, smoking, overweight, typical risk factors for heart disease. The shock of the deaths in my family reinforced my conviction that I must exercise the most important muscle in my body—my heart.

Five- and ten-mile runs, heavy-duty marathon training, became my routine. Put away were the collections of stamps; exercise had become my hobby. If I had two hours after work, I'd spend it training. Later, I began training before work, adding tennis and seven-mile bike rides before punching in. Soon, I started lunchtime workouts as well. Then I added swimming to the long-distance biking. By 1980, ten years after I had looked in the mirror with dissatisfaction, I was doing two or three workouts each day plus weekend training. Exercise was relaxation.

I trained for eight years before I entered a race: I was running for the health of it. My first race was a half marathon, my second a marathon and my fourth a 60-mile ultramarathon run from Philadelphia to Atlantic City. The more distance I ran, the more comfortable I was with it. No speed, but there was a fullness to the slower pace.

At work I put in ten-hour days. Thirty people reported to me; I had much responsibility and endless paperwork. I typically took on as much as I could do; DuPont was very fair in salary and promotions. But at the end of the day I could feel my face muscles tense. After twelve years behind a desk, I didn't know what was going on in the world around me. What would I have to look back on in sixty years? Would I have designed a petrochemical plant? An atomic energy plant? What would I have to show for my existence on earth?

Then in 1981, I decided to enter a planned transcontinental race, coast to coast, 3500 miles, 77 days, 46 miles per day, almost two marathons a day. I would have to train full time. When my leave-of-absence request was denied, I resigned. I was a bachelor with a few dollars saved. No one was waiting for me to put bread on the table. At age thirty-three I became a full-time amateur runner. I spent ten hours a day running, walking, swimming, stretching, weight training.

Pain and solitude are great teachers. I began to realize that all I had done was trade wing tips for track shoes and that competitive running was not really what I wanted. When the transcontinental race was canceled, I was out on the street with nowhere to run.

But the same factors that had put me on the street also gave me direction. What better marriage than to join health, exercise and work? But this time everybody's health, not just my own. Why not tour the United States to fight cardiovascular disease, the killer that claims the lives of a million Americans each year? Newspapers, radio, magazines and television all tell us to exercise to protect our hearts. But fully half of all Americans don't. How could I make a difference? I could look people in the eyes and tell them face to face: "Exercise to protect your heart." I could be a role model.

I started the Foundation for the Development of Cardiovascular Health.

Introduction

The foundation's first program was the Run for American Youth in 1982. A hundred or so pedestrians had hoofed the east-west span of our country, but I needed to do something different. No one had circumnavigated the country. That 10,000-mile path also intersected our largest population areas. With school appointments and major assembly programs in 37 states, precisely scheduled well in advance, I charted my city-to-city itinerary.

With road maps sprawled across my desk, I plotted cities and noninterstate highway routes on a perimeter course. South from the White House to Florida in the fall of 1982, west across Texas to California, up the Pacific coast to Seattle, east through Montana and Minnesota, New England, New York, and back to Washington, D.C., in the summer of 1983.

Road support would be one man in a stripped van, Eric Conrad, bike racer and photographic technician. All expenses paid, no salary for both of us. My support man resigned from the tour in Oregon, and I walked back across the country alone, having packed only necessities into a little waist pack: waterproof clothes, gloves, socks, a face shield and hood, foot care products, road maps and traveler's checks. Four pounds' worth of worldly possessions.

My program—consisting of talks and a slide presentation—was meant to supplement existing school programs and to motivate students to maintain a lifestyle that would keep them healthy. If children are given the knowledge and choice to keep themselves physically fit, they may not have to wait until they are out-of-shape adults to understand the penalties they might pay. I have been surprised on my trips to find that many adults have never seen the damage smoking, a high-fat diet or lack of exercise can do to the body's blood vessels. The presentations are often an education for them, too. My emphasis was on the things that affect children's health, the youth risk factors of smoking, high blood pressure, lack of exercise and overweight—the critical factors identified in the highly acclaimed Framingham Study on heart disease.

I started this tour on October 9, 1982. An experienced and conditioned ultramarathoner, I was putting in a hectic 38 miles a day. But by Florida, one month into the tour, I had 30 blisters and tight leg muscles. By Texas, 3500 miles after starting, I could no longer run. I switched to walking to save my feet and legs. That first tour taught me the value of walking when, at the end, I realized I had walked more than 9000 miles without any of the injury, pain or stress associated with running.

Introduction

It soon became clear to me that running, as much as I loved it, was not going to be the road to a healthy heart for the vast majority of Americans. It was simply too strenuous and prone to cause injury. And as I toured the country that first time, talking to Americans from every walk of life, I saw that running was not the choice exercise for middle-aged and older people, children, those with weight problems and many others.

This led to "The 50/50 Walk for the Health of It," 50 states in 50 weeks. Enter Gore-Tex and Rockport. It took a year to plan, mapping out the roads, calculating mileage, studying weather averages. More than one hundred walking events and school presentations were scheduled before my feet hit the ground on September 7, 1984.

The big difference between this second walk and the first walk is that I have learned the importance of walking as exercise, the universal exercise. This time the journey is being made at about four miles an hour, 32 miles a day, a marathon and a quarter.

We decided to expand upon the research Dr. Neeves had done on the first walk. The University of Massachusetts Medical School Center for Health, Fitness and Human Performance and the university's Department of Exercise Science and Nutrition would study me. Nine times during the walk I would be flown to U. Mass. for a day crammed with tests: treadmill stress testing, fat determinations, muscle strength testing, heart geometry evaluations, respiratory function evaluations, metabolism checks and blood chemistry analysis. All this research was aimed at answering the basic question: How does low-intensity, easy-gaited walking affect the total human body?

The major sponsors of the walk, The Rockport Company and W. L. Gore and Associates, were eager to learn how well their products performed under severe wear and weather conditions, so the walk also served as research for them.

There are 50 to 60 million fitness walkers in this country, compared to 15 to 20 million joggers. It is important to us to determine just how walking benefits the body.

This journey started in Newark, Delaware, and headed west, across the middle western states, down the Pacific coast, across the South, up into the lower middle western states, back down to Louisiana and Florida, up

◀ *A key element of Rob's trek was his hundreds of school assemblies on health and fitness. At the Roosevelt Elementary School in San Francisco, over 600 students listened attentively.* Photo by Fred Smith Associates.

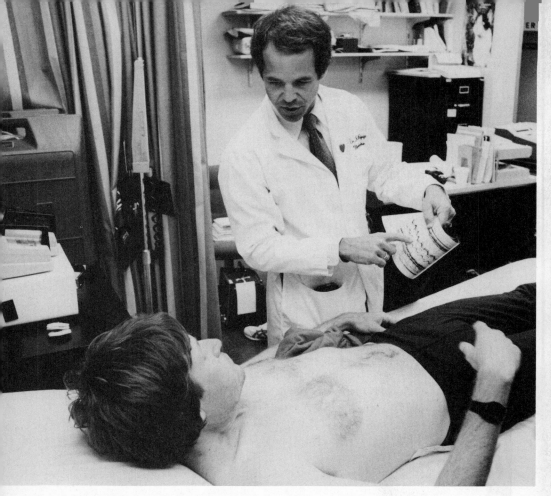

Dr. James Rippe, cardiologist and medical director of the
University of Massachusetts Medical School Center of
Health, Fitness and Human Performance (CHFHP),
explains an echocardiogram printout of the heart's
geometry to Rob. Rob was closely monitored by CHFHP and
by the Exercise Physiology Laboratory Department of
Exercise Science of the University of Massachusetts,
Amherst, throughout his 50-week journey through all 50
states. Photo by Chuck Kidd.

A University of Massachusetts Medical School Center ▶
technician bounces sonar beams off Sweetgall's heart to
check wall thickness and pumping chambers.

the eastern coast into New England and back down to New York. If a map of the tour were superimposed on the continental United States, it would look something like a melted eyeglass frame. I also took one-day trips to Alaska and Hawaii. Florida at a couple of hours is the quickest state to tour. California at 31 days is the longest.

My suitcase is a giant squash-shaped waist pack, zippered the full length and with an adjustable belt buckle that straps at the waist. A blue canvas shell, it is not waterproof, so all papers are wrapped in plastic. Fully stuffed, it weighs about five pounds. It contains antifungal foot powder, rubbing alcohol for cleaning skin, tetracycline for sore throats, Lomotil for intestinal cramps, aspirin for inflammations, petroleum jelly as a foot and thigh lubricant, and Bag Balm for dried, cracked skin. There also is lanolin cream for moisturizing the feet, sun block, a hypodermic syringe to drain blisters, a scalpel for minor skin operations, tape, bandages, adhesive pads, lamb's wool, a razor and one ounce of shampoo.

I also carry road maps that have been sliced to minimum size, a detailed itinerary of scheduled appointments, a sheet of news media and citizen contacts, a journal of long sheets of paper that are mailed home regularly, research data sheets that are mailed to U. Mass., press releases and newspaper articles (often the best form of identification) and, last but not least, my driver's license.

Inside the pockets of my walking suit or inside the waist pack are six pairs of cotton/nylon ankle socks, two pairs of Gore-Tex socks, one pair of Gore-Tex mittens and a Gore-Tex balaclava. Packed or on my body are an all-weather Gore-Tex walking suit (pants and jacket), one pair of wool tights, one long-sleeved wool jersey, one pair of wool shorts, one pair of briefs, one pair of Rockport walking shoes, a sun visor, a wool cap and pile mittens. Socks and other clothing and new shoes are mailed to post offices ahead of me about every two weeks, and many times it is only through the efforts of postmasters who stay late or come in on their time off that I am able to be resupplied.

The clothes weigh about six pounds, the waist pack about five pounds, one day's food supply weighs about four pounds. I weigh about 165 pounds, and all of us together weigh about 180 pounds.

This time there is no backup support. I came alone. Where I sleep and

On his 11,600-mile trek across the country, Rob traveled ▶ light, using only a five-pound waist pack to carry his essential needs. Photo by Chicago *Daily Herald.*

sometimes what I eat depend on the grace of God and the goodness of people like Dorlene and Ken Boulten in Worden, Montana. Expenses are paid, but finances are tight. I am always asked how much I'm being paid. I am not paid; I receive no salary. There is no charge for the presentations. Part of what I want to say is that there is more to life than money, and good health does not need to be related to money. Doing this on foot, by myself, without pay is what captures the imagination of the American public—one man alone visiting America with a message of health.

Sometimes I wonder how something as simple as a walk could have gotten so complicated. It looks like a Johnny Appleseed stroll, but it isn't. There are more than two hundred people and agencies involved— corporations, sponsors, hospital staffs around the country, families, school staffs. But in the end, it all hinges on putting one foot in front of the other and moving. One step at a time.

I usually get up between 4:30 and 6:00 A.M., depending on what time I go to bed and whether I am staying with someone who agrees to wake me or have to depend on my watch alarm. Between walking and talking with people, I manage about five hours of sleep a night.

I have slept on Persian rugs, hardwood floors, cots, couches, sleeping bags and even beds. In Northwood, New Hampshire, I slept on three dining-room tables pushed together at Angie's Stone Baked Pizza. In Norwalk, Connecticut, I slept in a $100,000 fire truck, the doors open to accommodate my head and legs. Throughout the two trips hundreds of people have been kind enough to let me walk into their lives and eat supper with their families and stay in their homes. In Taylorstown, Pennsylvania, Mr. and Mrs. Walter Grouse put me up even though they were celebrating their fiftieth wedding anniversary. At the Copley Plaza Hotel in Boston, I was given a $250 suite with a basket of fruit, wine, cheese and imported chocolates, all compliments of the management.

And then there were the police. It was dark and I was tired and wondering which way to step in Foxboro, Massachusetts. I got off the highway and asked the state police if they could put me up for the night. No—graciously—but they offered the services of the local police. A patrolman named Steve, the friendliest, most talkative policeman I've ever met, arrived in his patrol car to chauffeur me to jail—the best cell in the house, the juvenile block. As we drove off, I asked if we could stop at a grocery store for a moment while I bought breakfast. We pulled into a Cumberland Farms store. Peanut butter, strawberry jam and a foot-and-a-half-long loaf of buttermilk bread. We fought it out at the cash register,

Steve pushing my money back, me pushing his back. "I'm the law," he said, and breakfast was on Steve.

On the tours I have been pinned by flashlights and highbeams by police in every state. I have been helped and harassed, warned and advised, welcomed and cold-shouldered. I was mistaken for a jogging bandit in Arizona and questioned everywhere.

Wherever I go, I find that if I tell people right up front just who I am and, if I have a problem, just what it is, they are very helpful. "Hi, I'm Rob Sweetgall, the gentleman who's walking around the country. This is my problem . . ." Sometimes it is just a need to sit on their front steps and rest my feet. Sometimes it is to ask if they know anywhere nearby where I can find a place to stay. Sometimes I ask for a glass of water and end up with a bed.

Some people are friendly and open. Others are cautious. Most people are good about helping me in my search for lodgings in upcoming towns. They give me the names of friends or relatives or just people who they have heard are friendly. Sometimes they give my name to people up ahead. There have been a few nights when I have been walking in the dark, wondering just what I am going to do, and a car or pickup truck pulls up alongside and someone leans out and says, "Are you Rob Sweetgall? We've been looking for you."

Most people have a routine, and when I intrude, their reaction often is a welcoming one: "Glad you stopped, you really made my day" or "It doesn't happen every day that a cross-country walker comes by." A lot of people seem to catch the "I want to go too" fever. There is no age discrimination. The young, middle-aged and old all show the symptoms. Their questions are a giveaway: What advice do you give to a person who is considering a cross-country walk? Would you do it again? What would you change? What's the toughest part? Were you a top athlete in school?

One of the main questions I'm asked is about my feet. "Do they hurt?" Taking care of my feet is the start and finish of each day, a couple hours for massaging them, powdering them and using creams and lotions. When they become hot while walking, I stop, sit on a stone wall, front step or whatever is handy, and air and cool them. I get more than a few stares when airing my feet at restaurant tables, but I don't care. These two feet are my Porsche, my racing bike. They are my trip around the country and my ticket home. Besides, I must have the cleanest feet in America.

I walked into a town meeting in Garnavillo, Iowa, gave a short talk and asked if anyone knew where I might be able to find a place to stay. Doc

FITNESS WALKING

Sidney Davis stood and said he would put me up, but wanted first to know if my feet were as tough as horses' hooves. They aren't. Calluses build, but heat and moisture get to them, turning them into wet skin. Calluses come and calluses go. (More on this in Chapter 4.)

My appetite never tires. I eat about ten times a day, trying to maintain 4500 calories each day, double the amount a person my age would normally need. Brisk walking can burn calories equal to or greater than those burned by jogging.

I was raised a meat-and-potatoes boy all twenty-one years of my home life. After fourteen years on my own in Delaware, I converted to vegetarianism. Subsequently, I lost 20 pounds, all before the national trek started. When the perimeter tour started in 1982, I doubled my potato intake, which I had already doubled when I became a vegetarian. That's a lot of potatoes! After quadrupling, off came an additional 13 pounds. When the first tour ended, I returned to my normal double-dose potato level and ten pounds returned.

My love of potatoes comes in handy on the walk because I can get them almost anywhere. I also eat a lot of bananas (which have potassium and help to prevent muscle cramps), bread, peanut butter (a must because it has lots of calories), French toast (45 cents a slice at the Grand Cafe in Monona, Iowa, where the menu is painted on the wall), pancakes, ice cream, eggs without yokes (to cut down on cholesterol). I eat at lots and lots of salad bars, stocking up on peas, string beans, corn, carrots, broccoli, raw kale and spinach.

I try to eat at least every three hours to refuel my muscles. If I start the day with no idea if I'll be able to find lunch, I buy a loaf of whole-wheat bread and a jar of peanut butter and make myself six or so sandwiches to carry, tying them in a plastic bag to my waist. If I have doubts about the availability of water, I also carry a jar of water.

I record every ounce, half cup and cup of everything I eat and send reports weekly to the U. Mass. Nutrition Department so they can study how nutrition affects the body and exercise. I had used three plastic measuring cups held to the pack by a safety pin until I left them in Darian, Wisconsin. In Janesville, Wisconsin, I stopped at my first garage sale and bought a stainless-steel measuring cup. A bargain at 50 cents.

Rob receives the first of 78 packages of supplies and socks ▶
at post offices and homes along his 50-state itinerary.
Photo by Jim Fetter, *Pittsburgh Press.*

FITNESS WALKING

There are 15-mile days and there are 50-mile days, but there are no empty hours. There is so much to think about, to remember, to plan, and at least ten unexpected things happen each day. To keep myself busy on the road I have a number of games I play. One is called "Loose Change," looking for coins along the side of the road. If I think hard enough about a particular coin—a dime or nickel—I often find it ahead. On the first trip I found $63.30 on America's streets.

I improve my memory by playing "Recall," a mind game of thinking back over the past weeks, remembering details from each day. I started playing Recall during a 51-mile leg that stretched from the Emporia, Virginia, police station parking lot to Rocky Mount, North Carolina. I found I enjoyed it. I recall all the night scenes at early evening. Then I might recall schools or restaurants. After a while I could recall every single day of the tour and what had happened. Jerry Lucas, former New York Knicks forward, did the same kind of thing, memorizing the New York City phone directory during air flights to and from New York. My "phone directory" is the national composite of people and town names, road scenes, schools, blisters, emotions, phone conversations, cafe foods, motel rooms, police encounters, post office exchanges that add up to an unwritten diary of highway adventure.

On difficult days, I just concentrate on getting through that day. If necessary, I concentrate on the next hour or half hour. Sometimes I try only to think ten minutes ahead.

Much of the beauty of America on the road comes at the end of the day. I, too, feel the burden of a normal workday, of having to get miles in and things done. And there is a lessening of pressure toward sundown when the colors are leaving the landscape. It's a wonderful time to walk.

I have always had great respect for the weather, even before walking through Bozeman Pass in Montana in a spring blizzard. But the weather doesn't have to be dangerous to cause trouble. Hyperthermia, involving excessive body heat loss, is a problem runners and walkers can face in cool, wet weather.

In wet weather, salvation is often as close as the nearest beauty parlor. While my shoes were once dried in a restaurant bun warmer, the beehive-shaped hair dryers in beauty shops most often work best. The women and men I find there are always gracious and more than willing to help with dryers and free shampoos and haircuts. I am a better-looking walker for the experience.

Washing clothes is another matter. It is a little like the college campus fad of streaking except I don't move. I announce to those present in the laundromat what is about to happen so they can all turn their backs and close their eyes. In a matter of seconds I am out of all clothes and back into just the running suit while the clothes go round and round in a washer.

Loneliness is a recurring problem. Sometimes that pang is slight, at other times oppressively heavy. Thirty minutes is a light bout, ten hours or more a severe case, a day or longer a rarity. To me, it is a sign of weakening, of lacking inner strength, of being spoiled by pleasant company, conversation and compassion. An 11,600-mile walk can be a lonely experience. Fortunately, one doesn't have to walk 11,600 miles to stay healthy, and one of the greatest pleasures of walking is that it can be done in pairs, trios, families and groups of all sizes.

No one has to walk 31 miles a day for exercise. But I believe if I walk 31 miles a day, maybe you'll walk two miles. And if I walk every day, maybe you'll walk three or four days a week. And if I tell you how heart disease has affected my family, maybe you won't wait until you have a problem before you do something good for your heart—walk.

The major medical problem we have in this country is cardiovascular disease, disease of the heart and blood vessels. It is responsible for 52 percent of all deaths in America. The Framingham (Massachusetts) Study, started thirty-five years ago, clearly shows that heart disease is primarily a function of lifestyle. That means that most of us don't have to suffer from it. Such factors as diet, high blood serum cholesterol, stress, high blood pressure, lack of physical activity, the lifestyles we inherit from our families, smoking—all contribute to heart disease. Many of us have only ourselves to blame if we have problems with our hearts.

Smoking is a major factor because it influences all parts of the body. The Surgeon General says that 350,000 people die from smoking each year. If you smoke, you're six times more likely to have heart disease than if you don't. Nicotine and carbon monoxide poison the blood. It's like sucking on an exhaust pipe.

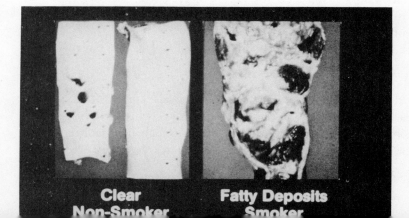

Clear
Non-Smoker

Fatty Deposits
Smoker

FITNESS WALKING

Look at pictures of the arteries of smokers and nonsmokers. Look at the cholesterol placque formations. A Korean War study showed that two-thirds of the soldiers killed who were studied had significant fat deposits in their blood vessels. They were eighteen and nineteen years old. My biggest offensive weapons in the presentations are 44 color slides showing the visual effects of smoking on the arteries and the hardening of blood vessels from fat-rich diets. Students and teachers say that they will never forget these pictures.

In a small town in South Dakota, a small nondescript cafe overlooks the highway. I stopped there to take a break and have a bite to eat between the miles. A reed-thin woman of about sixty-five, whose sagging skin told of weight she used to carry, wore short gray curly hair and a white apron. She sat drinking milk at a square table in the dining area in front of a pot-bellied, bearded smoker in a maroon jersey who was practicing pool alone. His gut and his Budweiser bottle rested on the pool table rail during each shot.

As I unclicked my waist pack to sit down, the woman asked without interest, "What do you want?"

"Eggs over easy, toast and coffee."

She dropped the plate in front of me with a clunk and went back to her milk.

"What are you up to with the pack?" she asked.

I told her about the walk and the children.

"What do you tell the kids?"

"I talk about exercise and why smoking is unhealthy and why . . ."

"That's my son over there shooting pool. He has high blood pressure and eats too much. You're looking at his exercise. You could talk to him forever and it wouldn't matter."

I nodded as I cut the yokes out of the eggs and pushed them aside.

"They removed half my stomach a while back. It still gets upset," she said and waited. "What do you expect to get out of this walking?"

"Satisfaction. I'm trying to help young people. If I can influence one student in every school I visit, then . . ."

"The way I see it," she said, "the kids are going to do what they want, no matter what you say."

I didn't say any more.

Studies show that strong examples, role models, are the single best way to teach good health. In the Oaklea Middle School, Junction City, Oregon, 54 of the 55 staff members, from principal to janitor, do not smoke. The state of Oregon is a leader in this area, having started a week-long program a few years ago to teach teachers how to be good health role models. Parents could have the same effect.

But who are the health role models for children today? The Olympic athletes? Football players? Baseball players? The only thing some of them are role models for is big salaries.

There's nothing quite like the thrill I get when children at the schools greet me with a roar. Even if health isn't the topic they most want to hear about, they might think, "Hey, this guy just walked 6000 miles or 10,000 miles just to talk to me." Life on the road fascinates them. What is it like to cross America on foot? What do you do if you get bitten by a snake in the middle of the desert? They put themselves in my place and want to know how I get food and where I eat and sleep. And they want to know about health. What are the best exercises and warmup procedures? If they do these, will they live longer? If they stay in the living room where their parents are smoking, will the smoke affect them? What do you do for shin problems?

When I began the 50/50 walk on that warm September day, 150 children from the Anna P. Mote school in Wilmington, Delaware, walked with me. One of them was Ken Wilson, an eleven-year-old who walked right beside me with a big smile on his face. I carried that smile for 11,600 miles. Of the 120,000 or so children I have talked with, if only one has been affected, it is worth the walk.

Walking is a means to health. There's no throbbing drum beat, no big sweat, no fancy packaging, no competition, no machines or memberships or expensive clothes. For so many years competition seemed so important, but now I have put competition aside and removed myself from races of all kinds to do what I feel is important and has some value. The appeal of "The 50/50 Walk for the Health of It" has been to the noncompetitive types. Exercise can lead to health, and good health is always ranked number one. The racing is within yourself, competition for a personal best, whether it is running a marathon, jogging ten miles or walking briskly to work every morning. What's important is what you feel about yourself and that you set your own standards.

If we lack health, it is hard to be happy and satisfied. But it's also hard to see that we might lose our health as we age. We accept the month-by-month reduction in our capabilities, the gain of a little weight ounce by ounce, the having to work a little harder to accomplish a job, the loss of flexibility, strength and ability. Sometimes it comes so gradually that we don't realize how we are threatening ourselves. But it doesn't have to be that way. We can walk away from it.

CHAPTER 1

WHY WALK?

I was eating breakfast in Selby, South Dakota, in a twenty-four-hour truck stop called Shortys when four old men (they must have been about seventy) walked up to me and started talking about walking. They go walking regularly, three or four miles every day. They do their morning stroll together.

As I was leaving Wautoga, South Dakota, population 29, at six in the morning, I saw two ladies about thirty-five or forty walking back into town. They were walking at a nice, brisk pace, too, about 3.5 miles an hour.

In Conowingo, Maryland, I walked into a meat shop, wanting to see what I weighed at the start of the trip. The butcher asked me if I was walking or running. He said he walked in his town of Rising Sun each day, a three-mile loop in the park there. I asked him if he saw more walkers or runners, and he said he saw more people walking, people doing two-, three-, four-mile walks, morning and evening.

◀ Sweetgall showing his bent-knee, easy-gait form, which he uses to walk at a 4-mile-per-hour pace.

FITNESS WALKING

Walking is the healthiest, safest way to start a total fitness program. It is the most natural way to build your fitness. As more medical studies of walking become available, the many benefits of this healthy form of exercise become apparent.

Each of the three of us came to our convictions about walking along a different route. One of us is a cardiologist with a passion for prevention who runs the largest cardiac rehabilitation program in New England. One is a physiologist who has spent a lifetime studying and teaching about the benefits of walking. And one is a walker who has spent the last three years walking all around America to bring the message of cardiovascular health and fitness walking to millions of Americans.

We practice what we preach. Each of us devotes a portion of every day to vigorous exercise. Walking is an important part of each of our fitness programs. But we have more than this in common. Shortly before Rob began his historic "50/50 Walk for the Health of It" he visited our laboratories for four days of intensive testing. We looked at every bodily system. We studied his heart and lungs. We dunked him underwater to measure his body fat. We used high-speed cameras to film his walking stride. We had him lie under a hood to measure his resting metabolism. We gathered up his inspired and expired air to measure the efficiency of his heart and muscles. Toward the end of the testing, one of the technicians saw the group surrounding Rob walking down the hall and exclaimed, "There goes Team Sweetgall!"

Indeed, we have become a team. Each of us brings a different perspective—the practical, the medical and the scientific. And we all share a common goal: to promote fitness through walking.

We are convinced that although you may have lived for years with an inactive lifestyle and developed some bad habits that can lead to poor health, you can improve your health by following a simple walking program. It may have taken you years to lapse into poor fitness, so don't expect to turn it around overnight, but if you follow the plans we outline for at least eight weeks, you'll notice definite improvement. If you get that far, you'll be hooked. Hooked on living a life with more energy and joy through total fitness.

A "thumbs-up" signal of "I'm okay" by Rob during the ▶
middle of a two-and-a-half-hour treadmill test at the
University of Massachusetts Medical School. Photo by
Worcester Telegram.

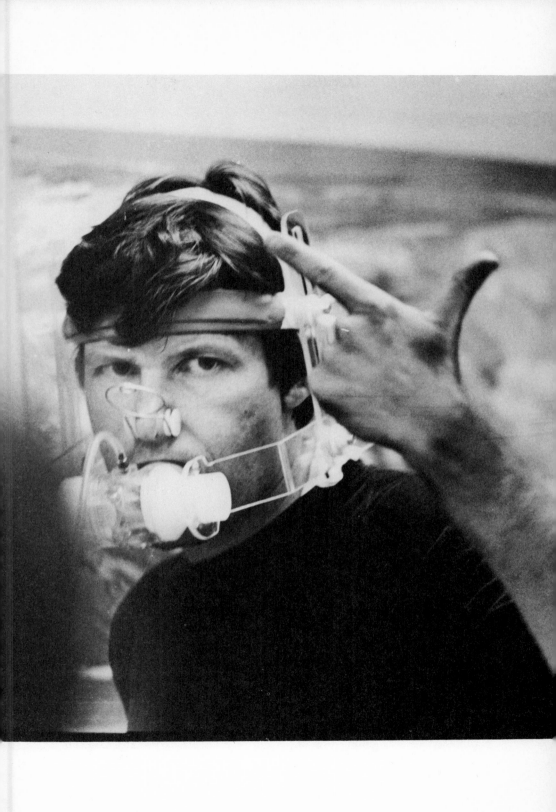

Health Benefits of Walking

Walking is quite simply the safest way to achieve aerobic conditioning with medically proven benefits. We'll discuss the medical benefits of walking in more detail in Chapter 2, but a few are listed below:

○ Walking is an excellent form of aerobic exercise.
○ Walkers are less likely to smoke cigarettes than inactive individuals.
○ Walking helps relieve stress.
○ Walking improves mood and mental function.
○ Walking aids weight loss and keeps the weight off.
○ Walkers are more likely to follow good nutritional habits than inactive individuals.
○ Walking slows down osteoporosis (bone loss), which may accompany aging.

Safety Advantages of Walking

There's a good reason why we choose walking as the basic exercise for all of our cardiac rehabilitation patients. It's the safest form of aerobic exercise we know.

Last year a forty-three-year-old pharmacist was referred to our hospital. At the age of thirty-nine he had suffered a massive heart attack. Fortunately, he was among the 50 percent of heart-attack victims who survive. His heart attack served as a profound warning to him. On his own, he stopped smoking, started following a low cholesterol diet and began a jogging program. Everything went fine for him for over three years. He felt great, kept his weight under control and, in general, approached life with new vigor and energy.

Then one day while jogging he suddenly felt woozy and passed out. When he awoke he didn't know where he was, but he managed to walk slowly home. When he casually mentioned this event to his physician, the physician became alarmed and insisted that he come to the hospital for immediate admission and heart monitoring. As we watched his electrocardiogram, we also became alarmed. He was having dangerous heart arrhythmias (abnormal rhythms). We urged him to undergo special studies in the hospital and let us find the best medication for him.

At this point he rebelled. "I've been following my own program for over three years," he said, "and I'm not about to stay in the hospital or stop jogging."

We urged him to start a monitored walking program until we could find a solution to his rhythm problem, but he adamantly refused.

About two months later we got a call from the emergency room at a nearby hospital. The young pharmacist had collapsed while jogging and was dead on arrival to the emergency room. Nobody would blame the pharmacist's jogging for his death, yet he had allowed his enthusiasm for his exercise program to cloud his judgment. He would have been safer in a medically supervised walking program.

What about people who have no evidence of heart disease? Should they be walking rather than jogging? From the standpoint of the heart there's no simple answer, although we believe that for most individuals walking is the safest form of exercise.

From the point of view of your joints, the answer is much clearer. When you run, you land with the force of three times your body weight each time your foot hits the ground. When you play tennis or basketball and leap into the air, you can land with the force of up to seven times your body weight. This is very punishing on your joints! How many runners or weekend athletes do you know who have been laid up for extended periods of time with joint problems? In one executive fitness program, over 50 percent of the participants who run have a serious enough joint problem to have to interrupt their training and/or seek medical attention every year.

If you're interested in an aerobic-conditioning program, walking is simply your best bet.

*Dennis Johnson and Danny Schwarzwalter postpone
building a cattle barn to join Rob for a three-day, 101-mile
walk through North Dakota. Photo by Ozzie Drager.*

The Myth of "No Pain, No Gain"

It's a myth that you have to exercise very hard to achieve beneficial effects. Those who believe they have to exercise until they are drenched with sweat are literally all wet. Many people have erroneously adopted this "no pain, no gain" philosophy about exercise. Yet numerous scientific and medical studies have shown that consistency in exercise rather than short-term intensity is what is important.

Some people feel that walking is not intense enough to produce the desired fitness results. They haven't seen people like Rob Sweetgall walk! When Rob was studied in our laboratories he was easily able to achieve heart rate levels that give the most benefit to his heart while walking at his normal speed. If your goal is total fitness, brisk walking is your best bet for aerobic exercise, and in this book we'll show you why.

In the past ten years, we've learned a tremendous amount about fitness and the human body. We know that exercise alone, even though it's very important, is not the only answer. That's why we call this book *Fitness Walking*. We want you to use walking as the cornerstone of your fitness program, but we're also going to share with you information and plans for developing total fitness. These are explained in greater detail in Chapter 3.

An old Chinese proverb says that "a journey of a thousand miles begins with a single step." That's a particularly fitting thought with which to begin your fitness walking program. You've already taken the first step by beginning this book. The next step should be just as easy.

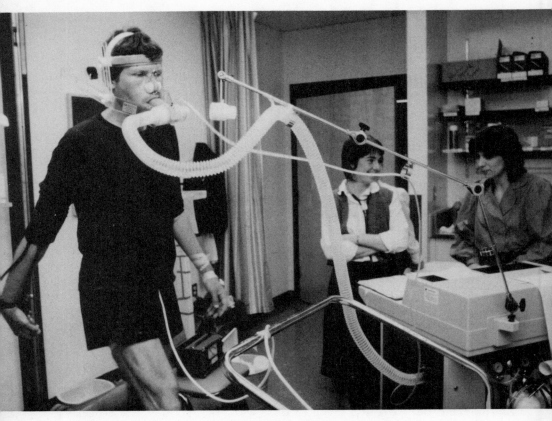

Technician Marion Gurry and Dr. Jessica Ross monitor Sweetgall during one of fifteen EKG tests. Photo by Chuck Kidd.

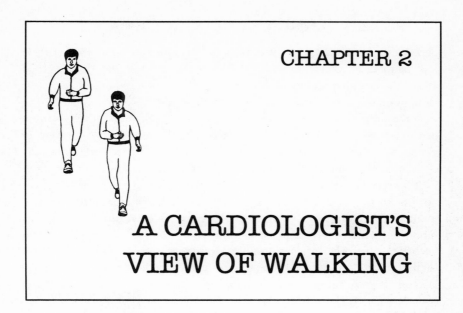

CHAPTER 2

A CARDIOLOGIST'S VIEW OF WALKING

It has been estimated that on any given day 70 million adults in the United States—almost half the adult population—slip out of their work clothes and into athletic garb and begin to exercise. And what's their favorite form of exercise? You guessed it. Walking!

This represents a startling increase from 1960 when only 24 percent of American adults engaged in regular exercise. It's also welcome news to a cardiologist, because if individuals exercise properly they may add years to their lives by reducing the likelihood of coronary heart disease.

Over the past twenty years there has been a slow but steady decline in the incidence of coronary heart disease (CHD) in the United States. There are many reasons for this. The incidence of cigarette smoking has declined, people are paying more attention to their diet (particularly lowering their cholesterol intake) and they are getting more aerobic exercise. When the National Institute of Health looked at the decrease in CHD (which causes heart attacks and angina), it stated that increased exercise was the single most important improvement.

But while we are heading in the right direction, let's not get too confident. The overall statistics are encouraging, but many Americans, perhaps the ones who need the most help, are doing nothing to lower their risk factors. Furthermore, many individuals who are deeply concerned about their health are doing the wrong things, not enough of the right things, or too much of one thing without proper balance.

For example, a friend of ours who runs one of the largest corporate fitness programs in America has a problem. Each year over 50 percent of the executives in his program (most of whom are runners) suffer a muscle or joint injury severe enough to interrupt their training. His problem isn't to motivate these individuals to exercise, but to teach them how to do it with proper balance and moderation. He knows that a proper program of stretching, musculoskeletal strength conditioning and some alternation with other forms of aerobic conditioning would keep them healthier. But most of these highly intelligent executives seem to leave their thinking caps at the office when it comes to exercise. They prefer to lace up those running shoes every day and go out and pound their joints and muscles on the roads.

Unfortunately, this is not an isolated group. At a recent Masters Track championship (a competition where records are set according to age group, with competitors between the ages of forty and eighty) almost 60 percent of the athletes had suffered an injury severe enough to interrupt training during the previous year, and these were often fairly serious injuries. Over one-third of those injured had been sidelined for over a month!

We're certainly not anti-running. On the contrary, each of us includes running as part of his personal total fitness program. In fact, we've all participated in marathons or ultramarathons. But the most important goal is *total fitness*. The central component of a total fitness program is aerobic conditioning. Some individuals can best achieve this through running, but the vast majority of Americans are better off with a structured fitness walking program. We will focus on some of the issues of running versus walking later in the chapter, but let's first look at the issues of walking and health.

Walking and Health

We have learned a great deal about the health benefits of aerobic exercise over the past thirty years, and most of the studies have been done on walking. In the 1950s two studies linked walking to decreased risk of heart attack. In one, London bus drivers (who got very little exercise) were compared to bus conductors (who walked up and down the bus aisles collecting fares). In another, postal clerks (who had sedentary work) were compared to postmen (who walked daily to deliver mail). In both studies, the walkers had fewer heart attacks.

Some have criticized these studies as inconclusive. "How do we know that the walkers weren't healthier when they started?" the critics say. The answer is that we don't. But even if the evidence is circumstantial, it's hard to ignore. Many other studies in the past twenty years have shown that exertion during work hours seems to decrease the risk of heart attack.

What about leisure time exercise? Here again, the exercisers have a clear-cut advantage. One study followed 16,000 graduates of Harvard College over ten years and showed that those who engaged in vigorous leisure-time exercise that burned 2000 calories per week were over 60 percent less likely to suffer heart atacks than their sedentary counterparts. These investigators didn't specify what forms of vigorous exercise were performed, but vigorous walking and stair climbing certainly qualify.

Despite these and many other studies that link walking and other forms of aerobic exercise to improved health, some critics still maintain that the conclusive study offering 100 percent proof that aerobic exercise prevents heart attacks hasn't been done. Maybe not, but we've seen enough proof. We try to start all our friends, patients and students on active walking programs because we have seen the benefits repeated over and over.

What Is Fitness Walking?

Simply stated, fitness walking is a total approach to personal fitness that uses walking as the major exercise. But exercise is only part of the picture. Total health means improving your flexibility and strength, paying attention to what you eat, and lowering your stress. The greatest benefits come when walking is placed in the context of a total fitness program.

What about other forms of aerobic exercise? Are they as good as walking? All forms of aerobic exercise, such as running, cycling, swimming and rowing, are good for the heart muscle. For most individuals, however, walking is the safest, most practical and most sensible core of a total fitness program, for several reasons.

Walking is a great way to clear your mind and reduce stress. This is one of the first things you'll notice. Taking time for a daily fitness walk will give you a break from work and a period to sort things out. It will help you think clearly and will reduce mental fatigue.

Walking will produce a fall in your resting heart rate. The physical benefits to the heart and muscles are called the "training effect." When you begin your fitness walking program, you'll start to notice this training effect within several weeks. Within six to eight weeks there will be definite proof of improvement.

Try this experiment. Take your resting pulse (see page 67) before you start your fitness walking program and then eight weeks into it. In both instances you should be sitting quietly, not talking or otherwise distracted, for three or four minutes. If you have been following the fitness walking program conscientiously, you will notice that your resting pulse has fallen, often by 5 to 10 beats a minute. You will also notice that your legs feel stronger, you have more energy, and you can accomplish more without becoming tired or out of breath.

The long-term benefits of fitness walking may take several years to achieve, but they are worth the effort. People who exercise throughout their lives tend to be leaner and have stronger hearts and more efficient muscles than people who are sedentary. They also live longer. No one has discovered the fountain of youth, but a lifetime walking program will certainly slow the physiologic aging processes. This has been shown in a number of medical and scientific studies.

Here we must inject an important word of caution. Exercise is not like putting money in the bank, making deposits early in life and then letting them accumulate interest for later use. In order to derive the long-term benefits of exercise you must continue to exercise throughout your life. Many studies have shown that college or even Olympic athletes who abandon exercise in middle age rapidly lose all the health benefits they had worked so hard to achieve. You have to stick with it. But once you begin your fitness walking program, you'll feel so good you'll *want* to stick with it for a lifetime.

Special Medical Aspects of Walking

Certain individuals can derive particularly important benefits from fitness walking. One of the great benefits of walking is that it is the most flexible exercise of all. Many individuals who have medical conditions that prevent other forms of exercise can still receive great benefits from walking.

Walking and Cardiac Rehabilitation

Each year over a million Americans suffer heart attacks. Unfortunately, about half of these individuals don't survive—many don't even make it to the hospital. Of those who do survive, many, perhaps even a majority, will suffer from significant disability following the heart attack. Cardiac rehabilitation programs can make a big difference to these individuals, and walking is an important part of a good program. All of our cardiac rehabilitation patients at the University of Massachusetts Medical School are placed on progressive walking programs.

Walking and Vascular Disease

Individuals who have narrowing of the arteries can suffer a variety of different symptoms. In the legs, this condition often causes pain and is called claudication. Walking programs can improve the exercise capability of people suffering from claudication and allow them to walk more with less pain.

Walking and Lung Disease

People with lung disease can accomplish more work with less shortness of breath after a walking program.

Walking and Arthritis

People with arthritis used to be told to take it easy, particularly when their joint pain flared. Just recently, however, several studies have showed that individuals with arthritis do better with regular exercise programs. Walking is an excellent exercise for most individuals with arthritis.

Walking and Bone Loss

As we grow older, our bones become thinner and more brittle. This is particularly true for women following menopause, whose bone loss is called osteoporosis. Walking is one of the best ways to slow down the bone loss process.

Walking and Obesity

Walking is one of the best ways to lose weight and keep it off. This is particularly true for obese individuals who are at high risk for muscle and joint injuries if they run.

Testing Rob Sweetgall

During his walk, Rob Sweetgall became the most studied individual in the history of American sports. People often ask us what tests Rob underwent and what they mean for the average walker.

Once every six weeks, wherever he was in the country, Rob walked into an airport and was flown back to Massachusetts, where he underwent thirty hours of intensive medical testing. These tests were designed to look at every aspect of his physical conditioning. Throughout these elaborate tests Rob was a real trooper. He was really determined to advance the science of walking.

Day 1

5:00 P.M. Rob arrives at Logan International Airport in Boston and is driven to the Center for Health, Fitness and Human Performance (Dr. Rippe's laboratory) at the University of Massachusetts Medical School in Worcester.

7:00 P.M. Rob eats a predetermined meal with known amounts of carbohydrates, fats and proteins.

8:00 P.M. Rob meets with scientists and medical doctors to discuss how the trip is going, any problems he is encountering and how he's holding up.

9:00 P.M. Rob goes to sleep on a bed in the exercise laboratory.

Day 2

4:00–7:00 A.M. Rob is awakened at 4:00 A.M. and placed under a metabolic hood. He stays under the hood for three hours, during which time we collect all the air he breathes out and analyze it. With these measurements we can determine how efficiently he is metabolizing his food and whether he is burning primarily carbohydrates, fat or protein.

7:00 A.M.   As soon as Rob comes out from under the hood, five tubes of blood are drawn. Some of this blood is analyzed for over 30 chemical values, using a DuPont automatic Clinical Analyzer, and part of it is frozen for future research. The blood is all drawn before breakfast, while Rob is in the "fasting" state.

7:00–7:30 A.M.   Rob eats a light breakfast of juice and Jell-O.

7:30 A.M.–Noon.   For the rest of the morning Rob is put through an exhaustive set of walking tests on a motorized treadmill. (See photo on page 50.) Each of the treadmill tests takes up to an hour. Once again, Rob's inspired and expired air is collected. This time, however, we're interested in how efficiently his heart and leg muscles are working. He takes a half hour between each test to rest and take care of his feet.

Noon–1:00 P.M.   Rob finally gets a break for a well-deserved lunch.

1:00–2:00 P.M.   Rob undergoes lung-function tests to determine how efficiently he is breathing.

2:00–2:30 P.M.   A cardiac echocardiogram is performed. This is a test where sound waves are bounced off various structures in Rob's heart and pictures are taken. It helps us determine if any changes in Rob's heart structure or function have occurred.

2:30–3:30 P.M.   Rob undergoes complete orthopedic assessment to measure the strength and flexibility of his arms and legs.

3:30–4:00 P.M.   X-rays of Rob's feet are taken. These help us determine the effects of distance walking on the bones of the feet. They were done only three times during the year to minimize the amount of X-ray exposure to Rob.

4:00–5:00 P.M.   Computerized tomography (CT) scanning of Rob's thighs. This is a computerized X-ray technique to measure the size of the thigh muscles and the amount of fat in the thighs. It was done only at the beginning, middle and end of the journey to minimize X-ray exposure to Rob.

5:30–6:00 P.M.   Dinner. Once again Rob eats a meal with measured amounts of carbohydrate, protein and fat.

6:00–7:30 P.M.   Rob is driven from the medical school to the Department of Exercise Science at the University of Massachusetts campus at Amherst.

7:30–8:30 P.M. Rob undergoes complete body composition testing. In this test Rob is totally submerged underwater so that we can determine his body fat. Another measurement of body fat is made using electrical impedance and girth and bone diameter measurements.

8:30–9:30 P.M. High-speed filming for biomechanical assessment of Rob's walking. Rob walks at different speeds while high-speed films are taken. Information from these films is meticulously recorded, digitized and fed into a computer to analyze the biomechanical efficiency of Rob's walking stride.

9:30–11:30 P.M. Rob is driven back to the airport in Boston and gets on a plane to be flown back to resume his walk.

As you can see, it's an extremely grueling testing process, but it's worth it. Rob's walk around the country offered us the unique chance to see a lifetime of walking crammed into the space of one year.

What did we find? At this writing, we can give you only preliminary results. A tremendous amount of data was generated during the testing, and it will take at least a year to analyze it all. Probably the most important change that we have noticed from early tests is that his total body oxygen consumption is over 20 percent greater than that of the average male of his age, height and weight. That means that his heart muscle has become stronger. He has lost fat (but not lean muscle) and the efficiency of his walking stride has improved.

Also, despite the constant pounding of eight to ten hours a day of walking, we have not been able to pick up any significant injury pattern, and he has maintained good strength in his arms and legs, which you too will gain as you follow your own fitness walking program.

This book gives you all the information you need to start a lifetime of health through your own fitness walking program. Before you start, we would like to give you some advice on safety. We were all saddened by the untimely death of Jim Fixx, the author of *The Complete Book of Running*. His collapse and death from an apparent heart attack while running has sparked an intense debate about safety in exercise. We would like to offer our opinion.

Before you begin an exercise program it is important to make sure that it is a safe one for you. The best way is to check with your physician. This is particularly important if you have allowed yourself to slip into inactivity and are out of shape. If you have an ongoing relationship with a

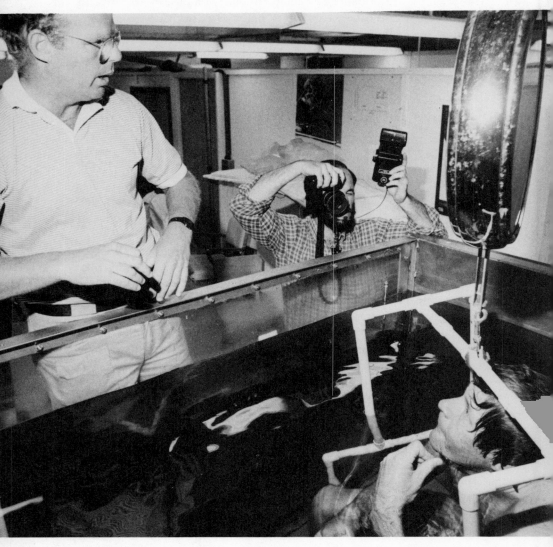

Dr. Frank Katch uses the lab water tank to determine Rob's fat content and body composition. Photo by Chuck Kidd.

physician, it may just require a phone call. If you haven't undergone a physical examination recently, this is a good opportunity to have one. In addition to examining you, your physician will want to obtain blood tests and an electrocardiogram. He or she may also want you to undergo an exercise tolerance test.

The Exercise Tolerance Test

The exercise tolerance test helps determine whether or not it is safe for you to start an exercise program. You will be asked to walk and then run at ever-increasing speeds and grades on a motorized treadmill. During the test, your physician will examine the electrocardiogram as your heart rate gets faster and faster. Changes on the electrocardiogram will help your physician determine whether or not there is narrowing of the blood vessels supplying the heart (coronary heart disease).

Recently there has been a lot of discussion about who needs an exercise tolerance test. In our opinion, any male who has been inactive for over a year, is over the age of thirty-five and wishes to start an exercise program ought to have this test. The same is true for any female who has been inactive and is over the age of forty.

Running

The running boom brought some important benefits to our society, but it also brought some problems. Let's look at running for a minute and then see how it fits in with fitness walking.

Running really got our society thinking about the importance of physical fitness. It also drew into a healthy activity a large number of individuals who had previously led very sedentary lifestyles. Running helped a lot of people lose weight and quit such destructive habits as cigarette smoking.

But there have also been some problems. We have already mentioned the stress that running places on joints and bones and the high incidence of injuries. Some people have even taken running to the point of serious danger or personal injury. Recently, the prestigious *New England Journal of Medicine* carried an article about "obligate runners." These individuals often run up to 100 miles a week despite serious orthopedic injury or other clear-cut medical reasons *not* to run. They are a small minority, but we all know individuals who run excessive numbers of miles and have long since forgotten why they are doing it. Even Dr. Ken Cooper, who popularized aerobics, recently stated that anyone who runs more than 15 to 20 miles a week is doing it for reasons other than fitness.

Perhaps the most serious problem with running, in our opinion, is that it virtually excludes many of the individuals who most desperately need to exercise. Too often, we've seen individuals go out and buy expensive equipment to begin a jogging program only to be injured or discouraged within a matter of weeks. Several national surveys have recently shown that the *average* fitness level of Americans has *declined* over the past ten years.

This is where fitness walking comes in. Very simply, fitness walking is the best exercise for conditioning for the vast majority of Americans. Even individuals who are dyed-in-the-wool runners would be best advised to alternate running with fitness walking if their true goal is *fitness* and not just accumulating miles.

Lifetime Exercise versus Short-Term Conditioning

The health benefits of exercise accumulate over a lifetime. Fitness walking is the perfect sport for lifetime exercise. The benefits of a short-term conditioning program are just that—short-term. Fitness walking is the perfect program for lifetime health through exercise.

Americans are becoming increasingly interested in their health and fitness. It is a trend that all physicians and other health care professionals should encourage. We believe that the principles set forth in fitness walking will make a major contribution to the goal we all share—a healthier America!

CHAPTER 3

THE FITNESS PROGRAM FOR EVERYONE: HOW TO RATE YOUR WALKING FITNESS

Part of the first cross-country walk was a walk through Brooklyn, my hometown. Out west in the rain, snow and chilling wind, I used to dream about the excitement of returning to my old neighborhood. It was not homesickness—that ended the morning after I left Brooklyn for good in 1969. The thrill was simply to see it again, kind of a sentimental thing, to rediscover how I grew up.

Something else intrigued me about the return—a chance for self-knowledge, to realize where time had taken me over the past twenty-odd years. Walking the old streets was like stepping into a time machine. I wanted to see all the little things that had been such an integral part of my childhood.

The concrete schoolyard whose walls of caged windows backdropped our punchball arena. The five sewer manhole covers that marked home plate, single, double, triple and home run in stickball.

Were the tire marks still on the asphalt from the '55 Chevy that hit me? Was the luncheonette where once a week I'd break from PS 138's cafeteria for a greasy hamburger, French fries and cherry coke ("Here's a dollar and don't forget to leave a fifteen-cent tip," my mother would say) there? The dark green and maroon canvas apartment-building canopy we used to try to touch while jumping? The trolley tracks that used to catch the edges of our roller skates? The pizza shop where my father bought me my first 15-cent slice served on opaque wax paper?

The actual walk that day made me wonder about sentiments I had felt out west. It just wasn't my town anymore. The whole perspective had changed. The sizes, the distances, the shapes, the colors, the store fronts, the schools, the apartments, the fences, the people, the vegetation, the smells in the air.

Everything was different. And so was I.

What shape are you in? Great? Good? Poor? Do you feel as if you can do anything you did when you were younger? Or do you feel you've lost a little of the fitness you had a few years ago? Before you start a fitness program you should have an honest idea of what kind of shape you are in.

The cornerstone of our system of fitness walking is a well-conditioned cardiovascular system. This means the body is able to deliver plenty of oxygen to the working muscles while, at the same time, improving the muscles' capacity to use this extra oxygen. This is the concept of cardiovascular fitness, more commonly referred to as aerobics.

During the first minute or two of continuous exercise, our bodies are powered by energy produced by reactions that don't require oxygen. These reactions are called anaerobic, or without oxygen. In order for exercise to continue, however, there must be a continuous oxygen supply to your muscles. That's where aerobics becomes important. If the muscles and cardiovascular system are poorly conditioned, the aerobic reactions cannot keep pace and you tire quickly.

There's only one way to improve the aerobic system for exercise and that's to exercise at the right intensity. We refer to that as the "minimum threshold intensity." If exercise is performed below this level, little or no improvements in fitness will occur. However, when you exercise at the right intensity for your age, you'll begin to reap the benefits of an improved capacity for exercise.

Before you begin your own program, you need to answer what seems to be a simple question: "Just where do I begin?" The answer depends on your present level of fitness. To help get you started, we've devised two basic methods to estimate the status of your heart's response to exercise. Select one of the two methods. While we strongly recommend Method 2, the first one will give you a rough idea of how you rate.

Method 1 requires you to rate your current level of physical activity by checking one of the five boxes below. Once you decide on your rating, you can proceed directly to your own program of fitness walking.

☐ 1. *Inactive:* You have a sit-down job and no regular physical activity.

☐ 2. *Relatively Inactive:* Three to four hours of walking or standing per day are usual. You have *no* regular organized physical activity during leisure time.

☐ 3. *Light Physical Activity:* You are sporadically involved in recreational activities such as weekend golf or tennis, occasional jogging, swimming or cycling.

☐ 4. *Moderate Physical Activity:* Usual job activities might include lifting or stair climbing, or you participate regularly in recreational/fitness activities such as jogging, swimming or cycling at least three times a week for 30 to 60 minutes each time.

☐ *Very Vigorous Physical Activity:* You participate in *extensive* physical activity for 60 minutes or more at least four days per week.

Method 2 requires your active participation in a three-minute step test. Consult your physician if there is any question in your mind about taking the test because of medical problems. If not, it's easy to take and you'll discover the current status of your cardiovascular response to exercise.

The step test also will be useful for establishing the appropriate intensity of your own program to ensure it meets the minimum threshold required to bring about improvements.

Step 1: How to Take Your Pulse

Perhaps the easiest way to discover the best location on your body to measure your pulse is to jog in place for 30 seconds, then place your fingers on your wrist, your throat, your temple or directly over your heart.

If you use your wrist, place your fingers gently over the radial artery just inside the wrist bone. If you have trouble finding your pulse, try inserting your fingers *softly* into your neck at the Adam's apple just below your jaw. Don't press too hard, for this can slow your heart rate and you'll get an inaccurate reading. A third method is to press lightly with the fingers on your temple. You should have no problem finding your pulse at one of these locations or directly over your heart.

Take a few practice readings when you are rested and relaxed. All you need is a clock with a second hand. You'll get a general idea of your resting heart rate if you count your pulse for 30 seconds and multiply by two to determine the rate per minute. For most people, the resting pulse rate falls between 50 and 90 beats a minute.

Step 2: The Step Test for Men and Women

The step test is an excellent, research-proven means for testing your heart's response to exercise. It is quick, and it is easy.

Suppose, for example, that three people perform three minutes of stepping up and down on a bench. Figure 1 illustrates the heart rate response of each subject during the three minutes of stepping. During the first

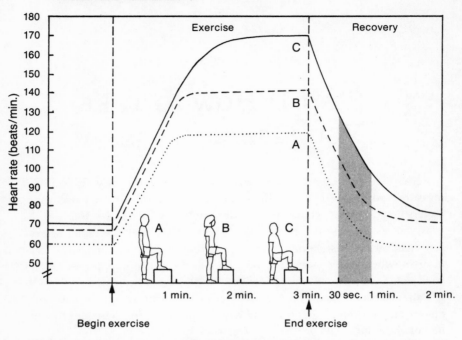

Figure 1. Different heart rate responses during the step test reveal different levels of fitness. As shaded portion shows, you take your pulse starting 30 seconds after exercise stops.

minute, the heart rate increases rapidly and then starts to level off. Subject A, a marathoner, reaches a heart rate of 120 beats per minute at the end of three minutes, while the heart rate of subject B, a housewife who exercises regularly, is 142 beats per minute. For subject C, a sedentary executive, the heart's response to the metabolic demands of this exercise is 170 beats per minute.

It is clear that the cardiovascular stress of bench stepping for C is considerably greater than for the other two, especially A, whose increase in heart rate is minimal. It would be reasonable to conclude that cardiovascular capacity is greatest for the athlete, less for the housewife, and relatively poor for the sedentary business executive.

Figure 1 also shows the pattern of heart rate recovery in the three subjects for two minutes immediately following the stepping exercise. Notice that on completion of the exercise, the heart rate decreases rapidly during the first 60 seconds of recovery. Following this period, the heart rate declines but at a much slower pace. After two minutes, the heart rate essentially has returned to a resting state.

The noticeable differences in the recovery heart rates of these three people are observed during the first minute following exercise. This is a good way to judge how well your circulatory system responds to exercise.

This test can be performed alone, but it is much easier if you have a helper. Find a stair or stool eight inches high. (You can adjust the height with boards or phone books.) You are going to step onto this height, one foot after another, up and down, for three minutes.

The correct stepping cadence is important in determining your heart recovery rate, so practice briefly to make sure that you step up and down *twice* within a five-second span, or 24 complete step-ups each minute. A complete step-up has four footfalls—that is, your right foot returns to the floor and so does the left foot. This process is repeated. You can have a friend chant, "Up, up; down, down; up, up; down, down," within a five-second span in order to establish the proper speed. Each new sequence starts at second 5, 10, 15, 20 and so on.

If you prefer, set a metronome to 96 beats per minute, giving one footstep per beat. You must complete two full cycles every five seconds— *no more, no less*—and you must do this for precisely three minutes.

Once you understand the cadence, either time yourself or have someone else signal you to begin and stop. Be precise, and do the step test for

---

Step Test for Men and Women

1. Stair height: 8 inches.

2. Cadence: Two complete step-ups every five seconds or 24 complete step-ups in 60 seconds.

3. Duration of stepping: Three minutes.

4. Time of recovery heart rate measurement: Start counting at 30 seconds after stopping and continue to the one-minute post-exercise period. Count the total number of heartbeats during this 30-second period. This is your heart rate score.

5. Intensity: About five times the "resting" metabolism. This is classified as light physical activity.

exactly three minutes. The moment you stop, keep your eye on the second hand and, exactly 30 seconds after stopping, measure your pulse for 30 more seconds. This will give you your heart rate recovery score.

Record your step-test heart rate score so you can compare it with existing standards in Table 1 on page 71 and so you can refer back to it during your program as an indication of how effectively you are getting in shape.

Step 3: How to Interpret Your Score

Use Table 1 to rate the response of your heart to exercise. Classifications have been constructed from average values based on a large sample from a representative midwestern community.

Keep your rating to help you determine the appropriate walking program in Chapter 5. Your starting point is determined by how you scored on the initial test. If you chose Method 1, select your starting point from the self-activity rating. If you chose Method 2, your starting point is determined by how you did on the step test. If you used both methods, pick the higher of the two ratings.

Your Self-Activity Rating	Your Step Test Rating	Page
very vigorous physical activity	excellent	124
moderate physical activity	good	122
light physical activity	average	120
relatively inactive	fair	118
inactive	poor	116

Table 1. Step-Test Classifications Based on 30-Second Recovery Heart Rate for Men and Women

CLASSIFICATION	AGE			
	20–29	30–39	40–49	50 & OLDER
MEN	NUMBER OF BEATS			
Excellent	34–36*	35–38	37–39	37–40
Good	37–40	39–41	40–42	41–43
Average	41–42	42–43	43–44	44–45
Fair	43–47	44–47	45–49	46–49
Poor	48–59	48–59	50–60	50–62
WOMEN				
Excellent	39–42*	39–42	41–43	41–44
Good	43–44	43–45	44–45	45–47
Average	45–46	46–47	46–47	48–49
Fair	47–52*	48–53	48–54	50–55
Poor	53–66	54–66	55–67	56–66

*Thirty-second heart rate is counted beginning 30 seconds after exercise stops.

Adapted and based on information in J. J. Montoye, *Physical Activity and Health: An Epidemiologic Study of an Entire Community* (Englewood Cliffs, N.J.: Prentice-Hall, 1975).

To improve hamstring flexibility, Rob demonstrates an effective resistance stretch on Bruce Katz, halfway through the 21-mile Continental Divide crossing near Helena, Montana. Photo by Fred Smith Associates.

CHAPTER 4

GETTING
READY FOR
FITNESS WALKING

Trust yourself. You know more than you think you do.

—DR. BENJAMIN SPOCK

Dr. Spock's advice to parents on child care is appropriate for exercise, too. In an age in which there are self-help and how-to books on practically every subject, we seem to have stopped trusting ourselves, our common sense, our instincts.

There is no trick to walking, and no one has to be an expert to do it. You simply put one foot in front of the other and always keep one on the ground. That might seem oversimplified, but walking *is* simple.

This is one of the reasons walking may be overlooked as exercise. It is easy, inexpensive and fun. Exercise—and fitness—need not be complicated, expensive or boring.

Mental Benefits of Walking

Studies show that walking has many health benefits. It lowers blood pressure, relieves stress, reduces body fat, increases cardiovascular endurance, strengthens leg and abdominal muscles, helps control appetite and improves the quality of your sleep. It will help you lose excess weight and keep weight down, especially in the legs, buttocks and abdomen.

Everything in the body that ages can be affected by exercise. Of course, walking won't stop you from turning thirty or fifty or seventy, but it can help make you look and feel better than you would if you didn't exercise.

Walking also has benefits not measured by charts, graphs, treadmills, cardiovascular tests and blood chemistry readings. These benefits include being active, well and in control of your life.

Americans have a lot of hard, fast exercise programs that reflect our hard, fast lifestyle. But walking reminds us of slower times, of peace and quiet and free time. Walking gives you a mental lift, a sense of well-being, accomplishment and pride. If you walk only a quarter mile to the grocery store, buy a loaf of bread and walk back, instead of jumping in the car and driving that quarter mile, you will have done something for yourself.

We live in a fast-paced society. Walking slows us down. It gives us time to unwind, to reflect, to plan, pray, talk or find quiet. It is a great way to deal with anxiety, tension, stress. Sometimes, walking is the only time we can turn off society, turn off our problems.

You can jog a mile faster than you can walk it, but is going faster what you want? Walking gives you time, a precious gift these days. Too often we look at exercise as a chore for which we don't have time. Time is money, we say, but what about life? How important is your body and your health? Time is health, too. Can you set aside a half hour a day to improve the quality of your life?

Open up your senses. Walking gives you something you didn't get in an office, or in a gymnasium, or at home. It gives you an environment you may not have known or may have forgotten: the outdoors, the sun, the air, the seasons of the year. Walking is more than an exercise. It is a ticket to appreciating the world around you.

Hear a coyote call in the night. See a deer stare off a hilltop, silhouetted against an orange sunset, listen to the rustle of the wind through the cornfields, the chirp of crickets. Smell the fresh-cut hay. Look at the houses and stores of your town or city. Consider the complexity of the urban landscape. Enjoy the architecture, lights, and buzz of the modern city.

Walking will give you that sense of relaxation and freedom *right away,* but fitness will take longer. Normally, it will be four to sixteen weeks before you start to see and feel some results from a walking program. According to a study reported by the *Journal of the American Medical Association,* improvement in physical fitness can be achieved in three to four weeks if a person walks one-half hour a day, five days a week, walking at a pace of 3 mph while carrying a six-and-one-half-pound load (e.g., a briefcase or a well-cluttered handbag).

People often overlook the benefits of walking because it does not build muscle. Walking for your health is *not* a program for muscle-building, though it will *tone* muscles in your legs, buttocks and abdomen.

Shoes

Almost 90 percent of all Americans have feet that are in suitable condition to walk three to four miles a day, according to podiatrist Dr. William A. Rossi, who is a consultant to footwear companies. Of that 90 percent, he says, most can walk with no problems at all. A small percentage may suffer problems such as foot fatigue, but they would have suffered these problems even if they hadn't started a fitness walking program. "Walking is natural. It does not abuse the feet. In fact, it helps them develop," says Dr. Rossi.

Podiatrists estimate that seven of every ten children and eight of every ten adults have a complaint of one type or another about their feet, from minor aches to severe defects. At the very least, 50 percent of those problems are caused by shoes, Dr. Rossi estimates. Studies of people in

Rob beginning a "foot care" stop in Tumwater Canyon outside Leavenworth, Washington. Photo by Nadra Rivers.

India, China and Africa who had never worn shoes found that only 2 percent had any foot problems, and those were caused by infection or injury.

A comfortable, well-fitting pair of shoes is the most important piece of equipment for a walker, yet there are only a few genuine walking shoes available. Many people have adopted running shoes to use for walking, but running and walking are different gaits and require different types of footwear for optimal performance and comfort.

Most runners impact heavily on their heels and rapidly transfer the weight forward onto the balls of their feet before pushing off with their toes. (Some runners land flat-footed, and sprinters tend to land on the midfoot or on their toes.) In the walking gait, there is a heel-toe motion with a moderate impact at the heel followed by a more gradual transfer of the weight to the ball of the foot. It is imperative in a walking shoe that it incorporate a reinforced counter design (for the area around the heel) to control the angle of the shoe as it strikes the ground. This determines how the weight will roll forward onto the ball of the foot. Combined with a curved sole (front to back) that supports the body's weight as it is transferred forward in each step, these features provide the optimal walking shoe advantage.

Although the cushioning in a running shoe works relatively well over short distances, the rocker profile sole and doubly supported heel counters in the most advanced walking shoes give much better performance in distances greater than two to three miles. Walking shoes also give much firmer support than conventional athletic shoes.

The Rockport Company, the first footwear company to receive the American Podiatric Medical Association's Seal of Acceptance, provided shoes for Rob Sweetgall during his walk. Rockport, the leading manufacturer of lightweight comfort footwear, has pioneered the new generation of walking shoes that are now on the market. Shoes, such as Rockport's ProWalker, are radically different from running shoes and have been engineered to control pronation and to provide the maximum comfort for the long-distance walker.

In choosing a walking shoe, you should look for a shoe that gives you support and comfort. A pair of bedroom slippers are very comfortable but give you no support. A pair of heavy work boots give you a lot of support but not much comfort. The key to building a superior walking shoe is to provide support at the heel and under the foot while maintaining the greatest possible comfort. When you are trying on various walking shoes,

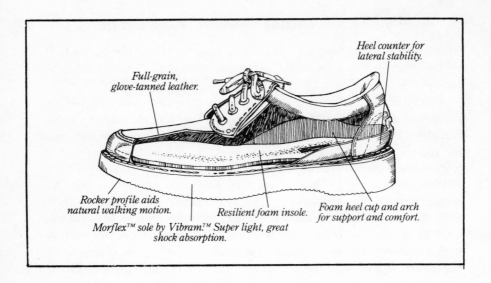

Heel counter for lateral stability.

Full-grain, glove-tanned leather.

Rocker profile aids natural walking motion.

Resilient foam insole.

Foam heel cup and arch for support and comfort.

Morflex™ sole by Vibram.™ Super light, great shock absorption.

be sure to walk around the store (preferably on a hard surface) for a few minutes. Also be sure that the shoes feel as good in motion as they do when you're sitting on the fitting stool.

In making your decision, consider the following.

Outersoles: The sole must feel reasonably soft when you push your fingernail into it. It must be made of a durable material and should have "bounce." You can gauge the "bounce" of a sole by striking your heel against a hard surface and seeing how resilient it feels. Many of the best walking shoes use soles manufactured by companies such as VIBRAM, which has made soles used on traditional hiking boots for several years. The outersole should have a rocker profile, which incorporates a sweep at the toe, to encourage the roll of the foot and to aid the natural walking motion. This enables you to walk without having to excessively flex the forward part of the shoes, allowing the shoe to be built with a firmer, supportive innersole. When the foot does not have to flex as much, there is a substantial reduction of foot fatigue over longer distances. A heel height of three-eighths to five-eighths of an inch will reduce the stretching of the Achilles tendon and place the foot at the proper pitch forward while walking. (The heel height is the difference between the height of the heel and the thickness of the sole at the ball of the foot).

Firm heel counter: A firm heel counter at the back of the shoe is needed to keep the foot in line. When you walk, your foot can tend to pronate, which means that the heel turns out when it hits the ground and the arch drops a little. That is the foot's natural shock-absorbing mechanism. The foot yields. If pronation is excessive, the arch will drop more and you will overpronate, causing foot soreness, fatigue and strain. A firm counter will buttress the heel. The more advanced walking shoes feature an externally reinforced heel counter that helps to keep the inside counter from breaking down as the shoe is worn in. Firm counters that are carried far forward in the shoes are one of the major differences between walking shoes and running shoes.

Internal cushioning and support system: The innersole works together with the cushioning provided by the outersole to cushion the foot's impact. Most walking shoes utilize some type of formed "orthotic," which is fitted to the inside of the shoe. The better walking shoes feature multidensity materials in these orthotics, combining a soft material on the top and a more resilient material on the bottom. The shape of the orthotics is determined by averages of the human anatomy. Each one will fit individuals differently, so it is important that you find one that feels good to you. Remember, the fit of a shoe is an entirely personal decision. In the more expensive walking shoes, you will find additonal shock-absorbing pads fitted to the underside of the orthotics that give added protection to the long-distance walker.

Upper construction: Walking shoes are made in both leather and a combination of leather and fabric. For the serious walker, it's hard to beat a leather shoe. Except for the open-mesh types of fabric, leather breathes better than fabric and will hold up considerably longer than fabric and leather. However, the fabric and leather shoes are lighter, and when made with a quality mesh material, can also give an excellent service. It is very important that you examine the way the pieces of the upper are stitched together. Any roughly finished seams will cause blisters and discourage even the most avid walkers. Also, examine the insides of the shoes.

Unlike some of the recent athletic shoes that are made with very soft leather, a good walking shoe should be made with a more durable piece of leather. The softer leathers may feel great on the fitting stool, but they cannot give proper support over great distance. Leather will naturally give a little in conforming with the shape of your foot, yet it should not be so soft that is will stretch out and lose the supportive shape that the shoe was made with. If your shoes get very wet, it is best to stuff them with newspaper and let them dry *slowly* at room temperature. This will allow them to retain their original shape and not become stiff in the drying process.

Box toe: The box toe is a reinforcement that is built into the toe of the shoe to keep the original shape in this area of the upper. It is critical in a walking shoe that there be plenty of toe room and a box toe that will not break down in wear. Any shoe that doesn't allow you to wiggle your toes freely should be avoided. A well-designed walking shoe will allow your toes to spread out naturally as you walk.

Weight: The overall weight of a shoe is a very important consideration. A difference of only four ounces can make a substantial difference in the amount of work required to walk even a short distance, such as a mile or two.

Socks

Absorbent socks protect your feet and your shoes. Cotton socks are the most absorbent, and the higher the percentage of cotton content the better. They do not have to be thick, and height is a matter of personal preference. Wool socks are also absorbent.

Each foot gives off about a cup of perspiration a day, almost half a gallon per foot per week. About 55 percent of that perspiration is ventilated through the top rim of the shoe, which opens to create a bellows effect when you walk. But about 45 percent goes into the shoe unless you have absorbent socks. That perspiration, day after day, will eat into the insole and lining, causing them to become frayed and worn. Two percent of the perspiration is salts and acid, which have a corrosive effect on shoes. Insole edges can become dry and crack, curling up and making the insole very uncomfortable for the foot.

Perspiration also makes the foot itchy and rashy, if not absorbed into the sock. A combination of heat, perspiration and pressure between the toes can cause corns.

Shoe Care

A pair of shoes should not be worn every day; it should be alternated with another pair every other day. This gives the shoes a chance to air out, a day to dry out the 45 percent of foot moisture they may be absorbing.

Once a week, loosen them up, opening them up as much as possible, and put them in the sun. The sun will remove a tremendous amount of unhygienic bacteria, which corrodes the shoe. Another way to dry out shoes is to use a vacuum cleaner. The suction works like a fan.

Foot Care

I have found that the most important thing I can do for my feet is give them air. As important as powder and lotions and creams are, it was airing my feet that allowed me to go well over 4000 miles on the 50/50 walk with only one tiny blister. And I have aired my feet just about everywhere, from guardrails on the sides of interstates during snowstorms to restaurants and people's homes at suppertime.

I was sitting on a front lawn by a row of hedges, just airing my feet in Maryland, looking to get a little relaxation, when a woman who was a passenger in a car signaled "Shame, shame" with her finger as she rode by. I never did figure out why she did that.

While at a table at the Red Rooster Restaurant in Reardon, Washington, I noticed a waitress looking at my feet, which were airing under the table. There were not a lot of people in the restaurant and I was sort of out of the way, so I figured there wouldn't be any problem with airing my feet. I always asked first if I thought it would cause a problem. Then another waitress came over and the two of them seemed to be making sure that, yes, sir, his feet really were naked. Finally, the head waitress came over and said I would have to put my shoes back on. I put the shoes on and left.

After I flew into Logan Airport in Boston, returning for medical tests at Christmastime in 1984, I'm sure many people thought it strange to see a man standing in the snow in his bare feet. But I had gone beyond feeling self-conscious about foot care.

When I was first involved in long-distance running I held the belief—which I now know is ridiculous—that pain was part of getting fit. I thought blisters were part of the price of training and competing. I accepted them. I had black toenails and toenails that fell off. My feet were red and cracked. I accepted it.

81

FITNESS WALKING

In a six-day race in 1981, I finally began to realize the importance of taking care of my feet—after I ended up with twenty blisters. Once I began regular foot care, my problems disappeared.

Pay attention to your feet. The more miles you walk, the more serious you have to be about foot care. It is not true that you have to toughen up the skin and get a lot of callus, or layers of dead skin, in order to walk well or walk far. You neither need nor want thick calluses. A thin callus will develop over a couple weeks, which is fine, but if it gets too thick or is uneven, it can lead to red spots, hot spots and eventually blisters. The red spots and the hot spots on the skin are caused by the friction of walking.

One of the most important things you can do to care for your skin is to give it air. If you are walking an hour or more, stop each hour, take off the shoes and socks and let air get at your feet.

Rob carried a waist pack, three-quarters of which contained foot-care products—his "precious cargo." That cargo included an antifungal powder, rubbing alcohol to use as a disinfectant, petroleum jelly for foot and thigh lubrication, Bag Balm (a medicinal foot ointment used mainly in cold weather), a lanolin-based cream moisturizer, spare socks, foot cushions, scissors, fast-acting glue for shoe repairs and a needle to drain blisters. Walking thousands of miles without backup support, Rob had to be prepared for any emergency. While you won't need a waist pack to walk a couple miles, you might want to take some supplies along in case of emergencies if you go for longer walks.

At a six-day race in 1981, a spectator told the racers, "Boy, it must hurt to pick your feet up after a while."

"No, it's putting them down that hurts," responded Ed Dodd of Collingwood, New Jersey, an authority on multiday racing.

To make sure your feet don't hurt when you put them down, wear good shoes, absorbent socks and practice foot maintenance.

Toenails should always be trimmed. They need not be very short, but they shouldn't be long. The more you walk, the more the foot stretches, and long nails can cause toe and nail problems.

Always wash your feet after walking. A very simple, very effective way to care for the feet is to give them an alternating foot bath. Fill one basin with ice-cold water and another with water as hot as you can stand it. Put your feet in the cold basin for one minute, then immediately put them in the hot basin for one minute. Do that five or ten times, then dry your feet with a rough towel.

The foot bath has a shock effect. The cold water tightens the blood vessels in the foot, then the hot water causes them to spring open. It is very stimulating and refreshing and is great for toning tissue and muscles and ligaments. It feels good after walking and prepares the feet better for walking the next day.

A foot massager and a whirlpool foot bath are two fairly inexpensive items that are beneficial for people who do a lot of walking. The massager will tone up muscles and tendons and, by doing so, will reduce fatigue. Massagers cost between $25 and $60. The whirlpool foot bath, which you can buy for $40 or $50, is also a great foot refresher and tissue toner.

Foot Problems

Sometimes it is hard to make people realize that a life's purpose rises and falls on 52 tiny bones linked by flesh, tendons and ligaments that take us from here to there. There are times when blisters will go away, but there are times when their effect swells in direct proportion to their size.

I had been limping, favoring an inflamed foot. The bubble was building and increasing pressure while I waited for the wind to die so that I could sterilize a pin.

"Lance it with the cold tip. Forget the microscopic bacteria," my wild side cried.

"Wait a minute. You're dealing with an open wound," argued the nurse in me.

Images of dark blue infected streaks running up the veins of my legs flashed in my mind, along with the hospital bed I'd probably be lying on, the tour cut short because of dates I wouldn't be able to make.

Mile after mile the frustration continued; all the time I was looking for a farmhouse with people, an open barn door, a driveway without a dog, a still pocket of air in which to strike the sterilizing match. How could any of the hundred schoolchildren that I had spoken to that morning understand these complexities of the seemingly simple, carefree life of a solo journeyman?

FITNESS WALKING

A teacher had asked, "How do you take care of blisters?" and I had responded in terms of cleanliness, powder, air, antiseptic and Bag Balm. But at 38 miles per day, 7 days a week, 40 straight weeks, my 60-second answer seemed such an oversimplification, an injustice to foot care. The subject deserved the attention of a whole book.

Who could have visualized me intensely searching for a quiet pocket of air in which to do my operation while preoccupied with debate on the bacteria issue. That morning, not even I had such foresight . . . the feet had been okay then. But slowly over the last miles, the red bubble had regrown its ugly head. What my foot really needed was obvious: rest, the unaffordable luxury.

Finally, in front of the rolling waves of a beige wheat field, there appeared a small white farmhouse. Desperate, I hobbled up the short driveway, knocked on the kitchen door, and was greeted by a small barking dog, that had heard me from the backyard. No one else answered. Dejected, I headed back out to the road. That's when I saw it, a corroded 1942 Chevy flatbed truck on which rested a huge cylindrical gray steel tank, my wind breaker.

The bed of planks formed the perfect operating table. The dog, still excited, followed me to the edge of the truck where I jumped onto the leeward side of the horizontal cylinder, imitating a gymnast mounting the parallel bars. The shoes and socks came off, the dog barked at my dangling feet and the operation proceeded, sterilization and all.

It worked.

Twenty minutes later I was a spunky kid, whistling a reprieve hymn of sweet notes of happy nothing while in full natural stride down the highway.

Never attempt bathroom surgery on your feet. Infections caused by trying to cut out corns (painful growths of skin) can cause many problems and have even led to amputation of toes. Corns are simply a consequence of the shoes a person wears. People who don't wear shoes never have corns.

For corns, ingrown toenails, plantar warts and bunions see a podiatrist and have such problems taken care of safely.

Walking Tips

There are no "techniques" for walking, no "right" way to walk. With the proper shoes, just about anyone can walk for fitness.

"The idea that a person should walk with toes pointed straight ahead is unfounded," says Dr. Rossi. "That idea originated from a mistaken belief that American Indians, great walkers, walked with their toes pointed straight ahead. That's a myth." A study by orthopedic surgeon Dr. Dudley Morton on foot stance among people in Africa who had never worn shoes found that most walked with their toes pointed out five to fifteen degrees. A study of college students at Columbia University found the same pattern. A little toeing out is normal. In fact, probably less than 10 percent of the population walks with their toes straight ahead.

Walk naturally. Don't try to adjust your style to fit some idea of what is the "right" way to walk. Excessive toeing out is a serious problem, but it, like other foot problems, will be obvious. You should consult a podiatrist, for many foot problems are correctible.

We can offer suggestions to make your walking program easier and to help you avoid problems others may have had. You already know the basics. Trust yourself. The golden rule is to do what's comfortable. Challenge yourself, but don't overdo it. That could mean a walk to the corner and back, a walk around the block or a walk of a mile or two to start, depending on your physical condition (see Chapter 3).

Exercise should be an everyday thing. Don't go out and walk ten miles just for the sake of doing it once in your life.

Recovery

The key to exercising and to every exercise program is *recovery*. You should never go beyond the point where, within 24 hours, you cannot go out and do the same workout again, whether it was a one-mile walk or a 15-mile walk. If you are so sore or have hurt yourself so that you can't repeat the workout, then you've done too much.

Posture

Good posture is essential to good walking. It helps you keep a good stride and improves oxygen and blood circulation. It also will help you avoid leg, back, neck and shoulder aches and pains that can be caused by bad posture. If you lean forward as you walk, a lot of muscles work to keep you from falling forward. Your whole body feels the strain and you will be sore and tired.

That doesn't mean you have to walk in a stiff-legged, rigid-backed march. When you walk, keep your back erect, your stomach and buttocks pulled in, your neck and head erect. Look ahead, not down at the ground.

Swinging your arms back and forth gives more power and distance to your stride and helps you keep your balance.

Take deep, regular breaths as you walk.

The combination of a good stride, a gentle arm swing, and steady, regular breathing allows your body the best use of its energy, and you'll move like a well-oiled machine.

Pacing

People want to know how fast they have to walk to benefit from walking. No matter at what speed you walk, you are exercising and your health is benefiting.

However, to get the muscles really involved and working and the heart pumping, a brisk walk is necessary. How fast you walk is up to you. Generally, 3 to 3.5 miles an hour is a normal, pleasant pace; 3.75 to 4 mph is a brisk, all-business pace; 4 mph is really hustling.

For someone on a rehabilitation program, 2 mph can be a fast pace. For someone who is very much overweight, 3 mph can be a burning speed. But for a person in generally good health, anything under 3 mph is slow.

There is no reason to go off in a mad dash, with arms and legs flailing. And don't walk until you are ready to drop, with sweat pouring off your face and muscles aching. It may make a dramatic television picture at the end of a race, but it's not a good way to exercise.

Distance

Get in the car and drive a measured mile. Then walk that mile, timing yourself. Divide the number of minutes it took you to walk the mile into 60 minutes. That will tell you your miles per hour. For example, if it took you 20 minutes to walk the mile, you walked 3 miles per hour.

The next time you walk the mile, count the number of left (or right) steps you take and multiply by two. That will tell you how many steps you walk per mile, another way to measure your improvement.

If there are a number of different roads and walking routes you can take, take the car to measure them. You can then make a chart showing the lengths of different roads or sections of roads. You can mix your walking routes, but always know how far you have walked.

Timing

When talking about walking, people generally use round numbers. While runners time themselves in hundredths, even thousandths of seconds, walkers walk at "about 3 or 4 miles an hour." It's interesting that few people walk at 3.3 or 3.7 mph. Yet there's a big difference between the two speeds—about 13 percent. If you've gone from walking 3.3 to 3.7 mph, an hour a day, five days a week, you've added two miles to your weekly distance.

Cadence

Everybody should find a cadence—a rhythm of steps—that is brisk but comfortable. It might be 125 steps per minute for a person with short legs or 100 steps for a person with longer legs.

Take smooth, long, even strides. It will keep you walking straighter, will stretch your muscles and will keep a rhythm in your walking.

Routing

Where you walk and what you walk on are important. If you can get off the roads and onto trails in parks or onto the shoulder of the road, there's a tremendous orthopedic advantage. You have greater endurance, less leg fatigue and fewer problems with shin pains (this is especially true for runners) if you are on softer ground.

But there is a trade-off. Footing and friction are less sure off the road than on. When walking on loose earth or clumpy grass, you can miss a step and turn an ankle. There may be holes, rocks, and tree stumps, so look out.

Try to pick a smooth level surface. Pay attention to how the road or path slopes from the center out. You don't want to walk on a surface that has so much of an incline from one side to the other that you have to lean to one side to stand up straight. Repeated walking on a road that is uneven can take its toll. Try walking different roads or on the same roads but on different sides or in different directions.

Surfaces

Grass, dirt, sand, pine needles, asphalt, concrete and crushed stone are all surfaces you may find yourself walking on at one time or another. The best walking is barefoot on grass or sand. It works and exercises all the muscles in the foot. But most of our walking is on hard surfaces, so try to alternate smooth hard surfaces, such as concrete or asphalt, with dirt or grass paths.

Clothing

Clothing is a matter of common sense and comfort. It should be loose fitting and appropriate for the season. In cold weather, wear layered clothing (for example, a turtleneck, a shirt, a sweater and a windbreaker). Layering helps trap heat and allows you to lessen clothing if it gets too warm. In hot weather, dress coolly, but keep yourself covered enough to prevent sunburn or sunstroke.

If you are out in cool or cold weather, you can lose about two-thirds to three-quarters of your total body heat through your head. Wear a hat. If breathing cold air bothers you, put a scarf around your mouth to warm the air before you breathe it. The hands and feet and head are the hardest parts of the body to keep warm, so pay careful attention to them. Gloves covered with large mittens is one way of layering to benefit your hands.

Persons on rehabilitation programs should consult their doctors before walking in cold temperatures.

Water

Drink water. It is a crucial nutrient for the human body. Drink before you walk, during your walk on hot days, and when you finish.

The effects of not drinking water were graphically portrayed during the 1984 Olympic marathon by a runner who missed water stops and finished the race delirious and near collapse.

Special Equipment

Basically, all you need is a good pair of shoes specifically designed for walking. One of the nice things about walking is that it is probably the least expensive fitness exercise.

A flashlight is a good safety idea for night walking. Some people enjoy carrying walking sticks. You can buy them or you can find a slim branch or stick along the road and make your own. They are useful for balance, keeping cadence and warding off dogs.

Exercises for Flexibility

Many youngsters have asked me, "How and when should I stretch?" Coming out of a rested state, one needs to have a gentle warmup that will increase muscle temperature to make them more pliable. Think of your muscles as taffy coming cold out of the icebox, brittle and stiff. Muscles can be damaged easily, just as taffy in this condition breaks easily. After a gentle warmup, proceed to a series of stretches that will further enhance flexibility. After exercising and a period of cooldown, stretch again to prevent unnecessary tightening.

A program to maintain or increase flexibility is a key element in any total fitness program.

A period of stretching before and after exercise does a number of important things. First, it allows the muscles and tendons to slowly "warm up." This is particularly important to prevent injury. This period also allows the heart slowly to speed up prior to the aerobic portion of the workout—an important safety feature. Second, following exercise, the stretching period prevents muscles from tightening up and allows for a gradual period of "cooldown," during which the heart rate declines to the resting level. Finally, stretching before and after exercising provides important time for your mind to relax and focus on exercise. We encourage people to focus on their breathing and relax during stretching.

Flexibility Tests

This series of tests involves three pass-or-fail challenges. Keep in mind that your performance reveals only minimal standards. If you cannot pass one or more of the tests, you have a problem with flexibility, but you may still proceed with a fitness walking program.

Flex Test 1

Sit on a flat surface, lock your knees, and see how far forward you can bring your fingers while keeping your hands next to each other. If you can reach past your toes, you pass. If you cannot, you may have too tight or inflexible hamstrings (the muscles in the back of your thighs).

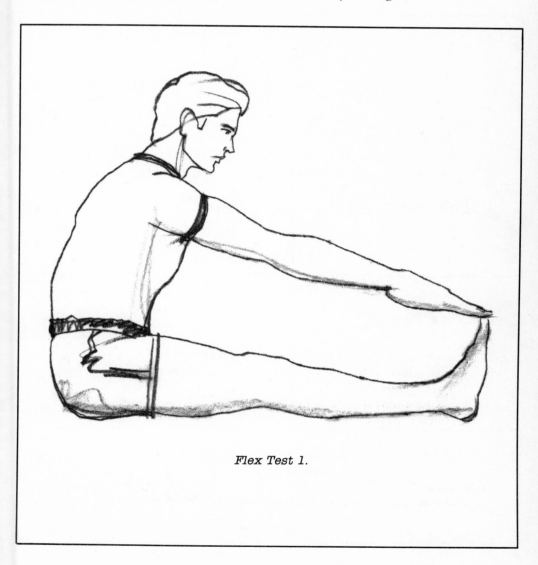

Flex Test 1.

Flex Test 2

Lie facedown on a flat surface and hook your feet under a chair or bed. Clasp your hands behind your head and arch your body upward. If you can raise your chin more than six inches from the floor, you pass this test. If not, you may have some lower-back muscle development to work on.

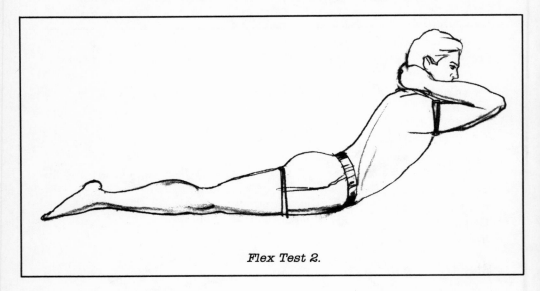

Flex Test 2.

Flex Test 3

Lie on your stomach and stretch your arms out in front of you. Grasp a straight object, such as a ruler or pen and lift your arms above your head. If you can raise them more than six inches, you pass this test. If not, you could have some tightness in your shoulders and upper back.

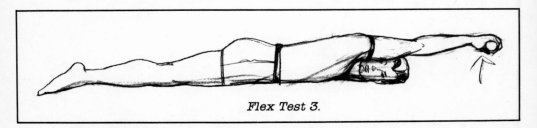

Flex Test 3.

Tips on Flexibility

Boundaries

Don't overstretch. Don't force yourself. There are always limits to what you can do. You might not be able to approach yesterday's limits today because the body changes from hour to hour. However, you will notice your limits changing over weeks and months.

Approach the limit of your stretch with respect. Linger at the boundary between discomfort and pain, but don't cross over to pain because you might injure yourself. Go into the stretch slowly and hold it for 30 seconds or more. You will not benefit by hurrying into and out of the stretch. The key is to stretch slowly without bouncing.

Relaxation

From moment to moment, try to be aware of the flow of your breathing. Take gentle, relaxed breaths. Try to relax the abdomen wall, which will allow the abdomen to expand as if you had a balloon in your belly. That will deepen your inhalation and actually make more room for the organs in your body.

Stretching and Breathing

When flexing at the waist, breathe out. When extending, or reaching up or out, breathe in. When you bend, you collapse the diaphragm, so to breathe in would be to attempt two opposite motions at once.

Awareness

Try to be as conscious as possible of your body, especially when you are moving into a stretch or when your body is reacting to a difficult task. Don't stretch mechanically or on "automatic pilot." Be aware of your body and what you are doing and be part of it.

Stretching

The human body needs to be used. Stretching is a form of nourishment to the muscles, joints, tendons and ligaments. It is a perfect adjunct to exercise, and is an essential part of fitness. A slow, mindful stretch takes only five to ten minutes, and it can make an important difference in how well you are able to exercise and in your body's total fitness.

Stretching is an important part of a walking program. Simple stretching exercises are covered beginning on page 97. Here are four other simple exercises that can help you in your program.

The easiest is a simple *toe raise* that strengthens the calf muscles, the major muscles used in walking because they give you push off the toe when you start each step. Stand straight (rest a hand against a wall or door frame for balance, if needed) and rise up on your toes. Stay up for a count of three, then down for a count of five. Repeat five times.

The second exercise is called the *crampy,* a variation of the traditional sit-up, but with less pressure on the back and abdominal muscles. It helps give you better balance, posture and less pelvic tilt. It also works the muscles in the face, cheek and neck and legs. Lie on the floor with your legs up, as if you were sitting in a chair. Put your hands behind your head and lace your fingers. Then bring your knees and elbows together, with your knees coming down and your head lifting up. Repeat five times.

The third exercise is a simple *leg lift* to strengthen the muscles in the legs and abdomen. Lie on the floor, hands at your sides. Bend one leg so that the foot is flat on the floor. Hold the other leg out straight, about 18 inches off the floor. Hold it for the count of six. Lower it to 12 inches and hold for six seconds. Then lower to 6 inches and hold for six seconds. Repeat five times with each leg.

You can use an old bicycle inner tube to increase the exercise by slipping one end over the foot being raised and the other end under the foot on the floor. Or you can use weights (available at sporting goods stores) or put sand in two socks, sew the tops together and drape them over the foot being lifted.

The fourth exercise, *toe rotation,* strengthens the ankle. Sit on a chair and stick one foot out, with the knee straight and the leg tilted downward slightly. Push your toes out so that the heel tucks under the back of the ankle. Then pull the toes back, almost in a waving motion. Turn the toes out to the right, then to the left. Repeat five times with each foot.

Students join in as Rob demonstrates "crampy-type" sit-ups—the simplest, most effective abdominal exercise that can be done anywhere without stress to the lower back.

These four simple stretches can be used at any time in your walking program. However, we recommend you follow a specific stretching routine that will stretch all the major muscle groups you use while walking and stretch the larger muscle groups first. Stretching prevents your muscles from becoming tight, gives your heart a chance to warm up and cool down before and after exercise and allows your mind to relax and focus on your walking.

You may need a few stretches other than those outlined in our routine. Everyone is different and has slightly different areas of muscle tightness. Feel free to adjust the routine after you've learned it. It's the same for all levels of fitness walkers, from beginner to expert. It should take five to seven minutes and should be done before and after each fitness walking session.

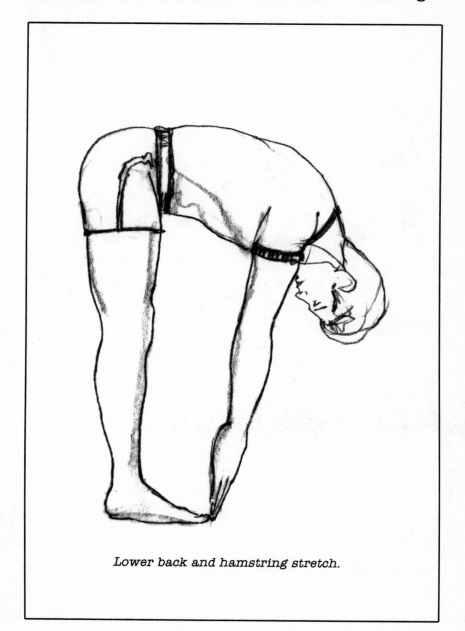

Lower back and hamstring stretch.

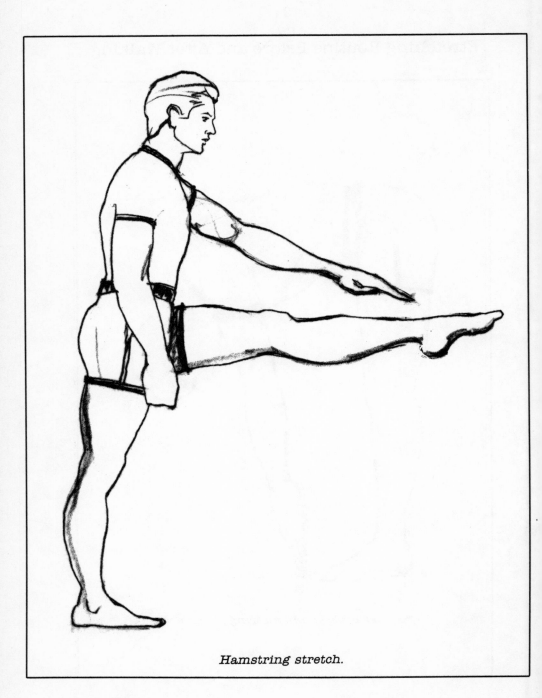

Hamstring stretch.

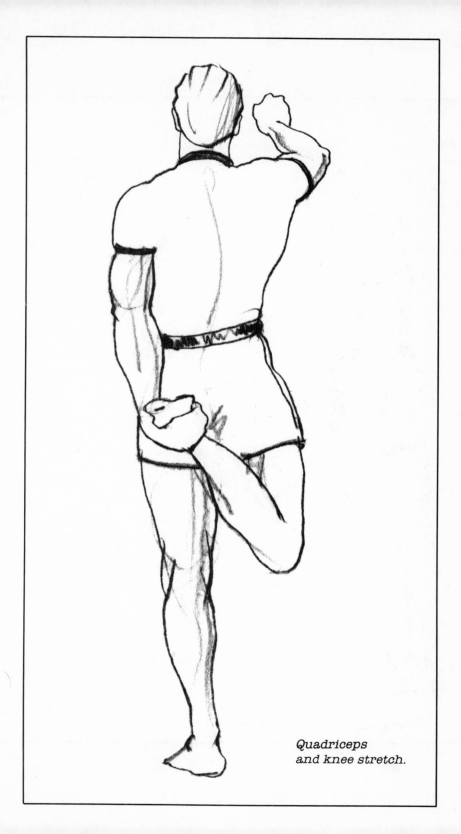

Quadriceps
and knee stretch.

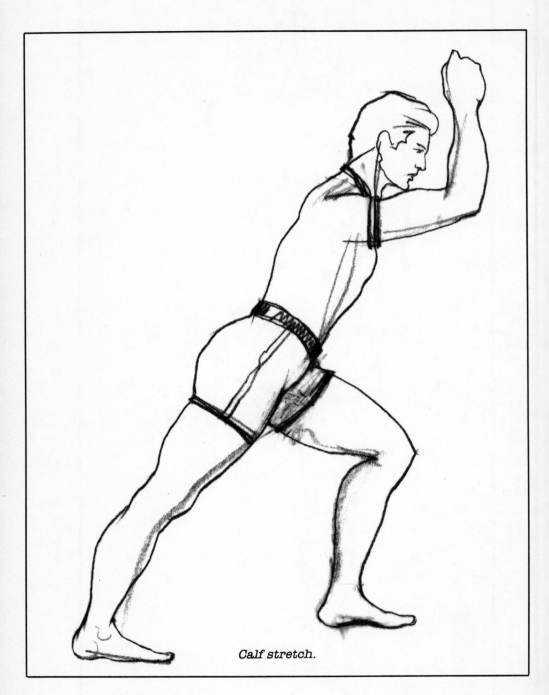

Calf stretch.

Shoulder and
arm stretches.

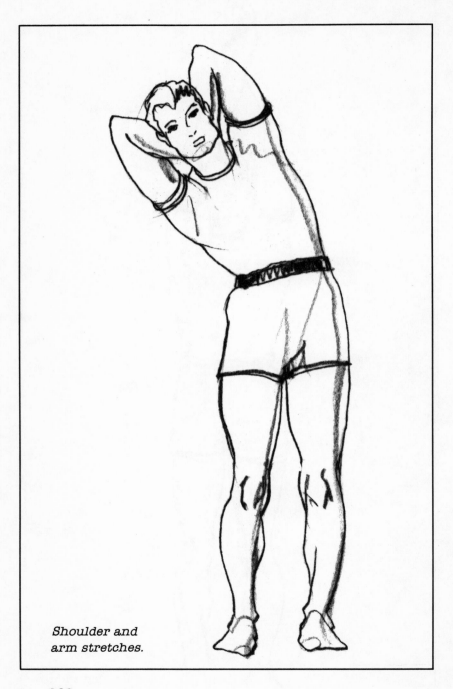

*Shoulder and
arm stretches.*

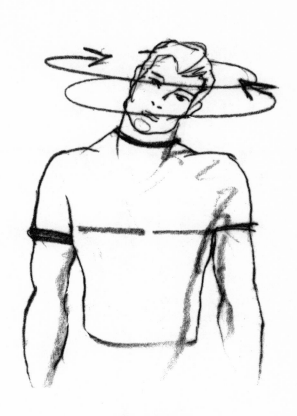

Neck rolls
(ten times each direction).

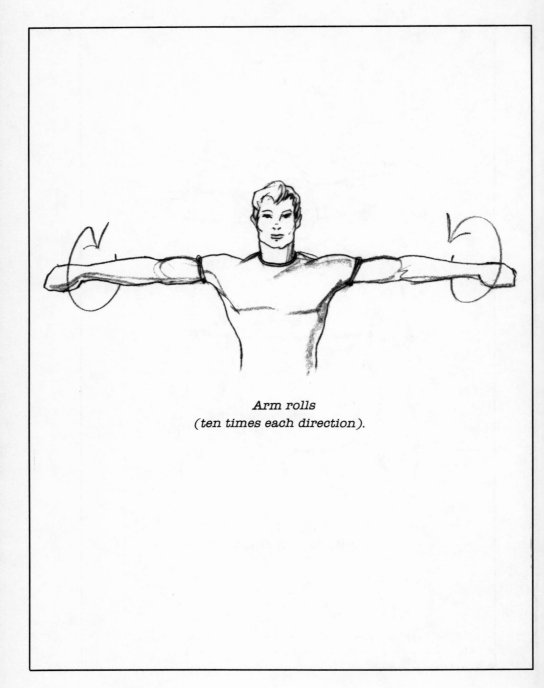

Arm rolls
(ten times each direction).

Strength

A renowned exercise physiologist once said to his class, "Let's put strength and cardiovascular conditioning in their proper perspective. You pick up the obit page of any newspaper and I'll give you five dollars for every person who died from lack of strength. How much are you willing to give me for every person you find who died from CHD?"

I tend to put more emphasis on aerobic conditioning. Muscle strength is important, and for walking, strong abdominal muscles are essential. The abdominals, in balancing the back muscles, control posture, which helps to prevent pelvic tilt and resulting back problems.

Walking alone will build your strength. Estimates have shown that walking power comes from upper body movement, i.e., the swing of the arms, forward movement of the shoulders, etc. Thus, upper body strength is important. During the second month of my fifty-state walk, one day in the physiology lab, Dr. Katch commented on the enlargement of my shoulder and chest muscles, asking me, "Have you been doing push-ups or weightlifting?" I shrugged and said, "No." It wasn't until the following week when I was buying potato salad in the cold Northwest and accidentally set my gloves on the electronic scale and found they weighed a half pound each that I realized that, in effect, I had been swinging those half-pound weights 30,000 times per day.

Strength and power have, unfortunately, not received enough attention in some fitness programs. This may be partially due to the old stereotype of weightlifters walking around flexing huge, ungainly muscles built up from years of "pumping iron" that are so tight they are barely usable.

There is also the opposite stereotype, the rail-thin, long-distance runner with virtually no muscle on the upper body and insufficient upper body strength.

There *is* a middle ground. We do not advocate building enormous muscles. However, we do believe that a judicious program of light weights or resistance exercises (particularly for the upper body) will enhance your overall level of fitness and actually contribute to your enjoyment of fitness walking. Just as in any form of exercise, it is important to observe safety precautions during weight training. You should check with your physician prior to starting. Weight-training exercises may be particularly dangerous if you have high blood pressure or coronary heart disease. Those individuals should avoid this form of exercise.

Muscular Strength Tests

These two tests we've selected to evaluate muscular strength are pass or fail.

Test 1: Sit-ups

This test evaluates the muscles in the hip and abdominal region.

How many sit-ups can you do in one session? Place your hands behind your neck. Keeping your knees bent slightly and your feet flat on the floor, roll up to a sitting position. To pass, you must be able to do at least 15 sit-ups before tiring.

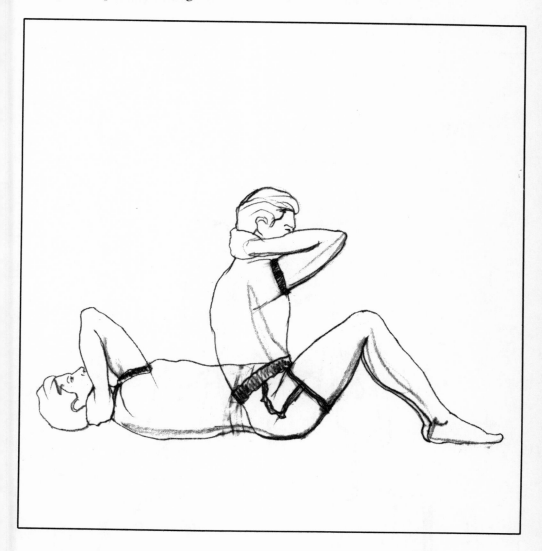

Test 2: Upper Body Strength

Place two solid hardback chairs about two to three feet apart (depending on your size), with their backs facing in. Place yourself between them, grip the backs, and place all your weight on your arms, lifting your feet slightly from the floor. After balancing yourself, you should be able to support your body for 30 seconds without your arms trembling. If you can, you pass.

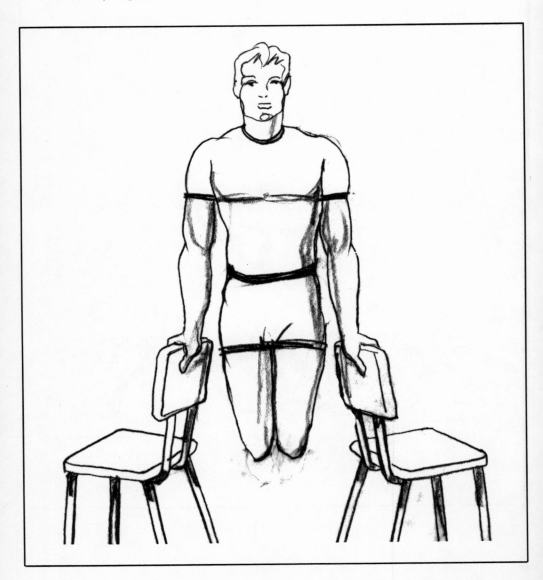

Motor Control

*Many sports and exercises involve strong hand-eye coordination.
Fortunately, walking requires only an easy, natural gait, and little
coordination is necessary. As I move down the highway, I do not try
to force any type of form that is unnatural to me. However, the one
thing I do try to concentrate on is my foot placement. I try to step in
nearly a straight line. I try to let the insides of my feet nip the edge
of an imaginary four-inch white stripe. Besides keeping me on a
straight path, this improves my stride length. Sometimes when
walking on soft earth, packed snow or crunchy ice, I will turn
around and backtrack a few steps to inspect my foot alignment. In
Preston, Minnesota, I was reminded of the importance of this as I
stepped into the local sheriff's office to find a place to sleep. After
being escorted into the visitation cell block, which was to be my
bedroom for the night, I noticed a black-and-white poster taped to
the glass viewing wall, showing a pair of feet walking down the
white stripe of the highway at night. The caption read, "If you
can't walk a straight line, we'll give you a month to practice."*

All of our movements, from the most delicate task of threading a needle
to the power and coordination in slugging a home run, are under the tight
control of our nervous system. Coordination and balance involve fine-
tuned integration of the muscles, joints and bones. The remarkable and
complex tasks carried out under the local control of the nerves are guided
by the magnificent computer—the human brain. The brain allows us to
learn from past mistakes and acquire new skills. Fitness walking is like
any other new activity or sport in which you learn new skills and perfect
techniques. As your body learns new and more efficient techniques, the
brain stores the lessons and helps you repeat them. This whole process is
what we call motor control.

CHAPTER 5

YOUR FITNESS WALKING PROGRAM FROM STARTER TO EXPERT

When I look back on this journey, it won't be the days at the start or finish that I'll remember. It will be the days in between, the days that sometimes seem to all run together, the ordinary days of walking and watching and thinking.

Every day is special. Every day I see something, hear something or realize something new.

And one thing I realize is that even though what I am doing is healthy and beneficial and important, it is also fun. For whatever other reasons I walk, I also walk because I enjoy it.

◀ *Roosevelt Middle School students join Rob in a post-assembly walking clinic through the streets of San Francisco. Day 153, 4500-mile mark. Photo by Fred Smith Associates.*

FITNESS WALKING

In this chapter, we'll help you plan your personal fitness walking program. Even if you are eager to jump right into fitness walking, take a few minutes to read these introductory remarks and Chapter 4, "Getting Ready for Fitness Walking."

Once you have learned how to do the proper stretches, refer back to the results of your aerobic fitness test (the step-test results or the self-assessment from Chapter 3). Use the results of whichever test you took to place yourself in the correct fitness walking category. The correlations are as follows:

Step Test Result	Fitness Self-Assessment	Fitness Walking Category
poor	1	starter
fair	2	beginner
average	3	intermediate
good	4	advanced
excellent	5	expert

Three things are particularly important to accomplish before you start your fitness walking program:

1. Make sure it is medically safe for you to participate.
2. Learn how to take your pulse.
3. Buy the right equipment.

Safety: The Preprogram Evaluation

As we discussed earlier, if you have been inactive, it is very important to consult your physician before beginning an exercise program. If you already have a long-standing relationship with a physician, this may just mean a phone call. If you have not received regular medical care or have not had a physical exam in the past year make an appointment to see your doctor.

Your physician will want to discuss with you any risk factors you have for heart disease (such as high blood pressure, an elevated cholesterol level, cigarette smoking or family members who have had heart disease). He or she will also perform a physical exam and obtain a cardiogram (EKG), and may also recommend an exercise stress test.

The exercise stress test is one of the best ways of making sure an exercise program is safe for you. The test involves putting EKG leads on your chest and monitoring your heart while you run on a motorized treadmill. By looking at the cardiogram while the heart is under this "stress" of exercise, the physician can tell if it is safe for you to begin a program.

Who needs an exercise stress test? We believe that any male over the age of thirty-five or any female over the age of forty who wants to begin an exercise program should have this test. Even if you are younger, if you have been very inactive or have high risk factors for heart disease, undergoing the test is a good idea. Of course, there are some exceptions, and it is best to check with your physician.

Learning Your Target Heart Rate

All serious walkers should learn how to determine their target heart rate to ensure that maximum aerobic benefits are achieved during periods of exercise walking. All of the fitness walking programs are based on target heart rates, so you must learn how to take your pulse and calculate your heart rate. The techniques are really very simple, but they require a little patience, practice and some simple arithmetic.

Step 1: Feel the pulse of the artery at your wrist (the "radial" pulse). Feel the pulse of one wrist with the fingertips of the other hand. Time the pulse with your watch. Count the number of beats for 15 seconds then multiply by four to derive the number of heartbeats per minute. For example, if while relaxing you count 18 beats in 15 seconds your resting heart rate is 18×4, or 72 beats per minute.

Step 2: Compute your maximum predicted heart rate. The easiest way is to take 220 beats per minute and subtract your age. For example, if you are forty-five years old, your predicted maximum heart rate is $220 - 45$, or 175 beats per minute.

Step 3: Determine your "target" heart rate zone. This just involves multiplying your maximum heart rate by 70 percent and by 80 percent. For our forty-five-year-old, the target zone lies between 175×70 percent and 175×80 percent, or between 123 and 140 beats per minute.

Step 4: Now, after stretching, begin your walk. Follow the upcoming instructions outlined for Week 1 in the category your fitness test placed you in. Spend the first few minutes slowly building up your pace. When you have reached a "brisk" pace, determine your pulse rate as outlined above. If you are below your target zone, speed up. If you are above the target zone, slow down. Once you are in the target zone, maintain this pace for twenty minutes, checking your pulse rate every five minutes. After you have followed this routine a few times you will be able to estimate your heart rate with fewer actual measurements.

Now proceed to the appropriate fitness walking category and begin your personal program. Welcome to the world of fitness walking. Enjoy yourself and walk in health!

The Programs

Each of the protocols was developed in our laboratories. Don't be intimidated by them. They are designed for you and will help you feel better and make your heart stronger. Remember, trust yourself. You know more than you think you do. Don't let anyone tell you that walking is difficult. What *is* difficult is changing from a sedentary lifestyle to one in which exercise is part of your daily routine. But you can do it! Make a commitment to yourself and your health. After two months of fitness walking you'll wonder how you ever did without it. We guarantee it!

If you are already a regular fitness walker, you know the pleasure of being in good shape and feeling good about yourself. If you're currently sedentary, a whole new world will open to you.

Starter Program

If you scored in the "poor" category of the step test or rated yourself as "inactive" on the self-rating scale, then the Starter Program is for you. You've got a ways to go, but look at it this way—you stand to benefit the most from fitness walking!

The hardest part will be the first several weeks. You may have not had regular exercise for years, so give yourself a chance to ease into the program. Make a commitment to yourself to stick with it. Plan a specific time each day for your fitness walk. Buy a good pair of shoes specifically designed for walking (see Chapter 4). Find a friend to walk with you.

Write down your mileage and how you feel each day in the log at the back of this book. This is very important and will give you a sense of what you have accomplished.

Remember not to take any shortcuts. Learn how to take your pulse. Make sure you do the stretches outlined in Chapter 4 both before and after walking.

The longest journey begins with a single step and you're about to start yours with fitness walking.

Starter Program

WEEK	WARMUP	MILEAGE	PACE (mph)	HEART RATE (% of max.)	COOLDOWN	FREQUENCY (times per week)
1	5–7 mins. before-walk stretches	1.0	3.0	60	5–7 mins. after-walk stretches	5
2	5–7 mins.	1.0	3.0	60	5–7 mins.	5
3	5–7 mins.	1.25	3.0	60	5–7 mins.	5
4	5–7 mins.	1.25	3.0	60	5–7 mins.	5
5	5–7 mins.	1.5	3.0	60	5–7 mins.	5
6	5–7 mins.	1.5	3.5	60–70	5–7 mins.	5
7	5–7 mins.	1.75	3.5	60–70	5–7 mins.	5
8	5–7 mins.	1.75	3.5	60–70	5–7 mins.	5
9	5–7 mins.	2.0	3.5	60–70	5–7 mins.	5
10	5–7 mins.	2.0	3.75	60–70	5–7 mins.	5
11	5–7 mins.	2.0	3.75	70	5–7 mins.	5
12	5–7 mins.	2.25	3.75	70	5–7 mins.	5
13	5–7 mins.	2.25	3.75	70	5–7 mins.	5
14	5–7 mins.	2.5	3.75	70	5–7 mins.	5
15	5–7 mins.	2.5	4.0	70	5–7 mins.	5
16	5–7 mins.	2.5	4.0	70	5–7 mins.	5
17	5–7 mins.	2.75	4.0	70–80	5–7 mins.	5
18	5–7 mins.	2.75	4.0	70–80	5–7 mins.	5
19	5–7 mins.	3.0	4.0	70–80	5–7 mins.	5
20	5–7 mins.	3.0	4.0	70–80	5–7 mins.	5

At the end of the twenty-week fitness walking protocol you may either retest yourself and move to a new fitness walking category or turn directly to the Intermediate Maintenance Program for a lifetime of fitness walking.

Beginner Program

If you scored in the "fair" category on the step test or rated yourself in the "relatively inactive" category on the self-rating scale, then the Beginner Program is for you. Chances are that if you're in this category, you do have some light exercise in your daily routine but don't set aside a specific period for regular, vigorous exercise.

Fitness walking will help you organize your time, and you'll be amazed at the extra energy it gives you. Don't be surprised if it takes a while to get used to the regular period of walking. It took you a while to get out of shape, so be patient with yourself as you get back into it.

Develop a plan to help you approach fitness walking. Be sure to do the stretches outlined in Chapter 4 both before and after each fitness walking session. Record your daily progress in the log at the end of the book. By the end of the twenty weeks you'll be ready to move into one of the more advanced protocols.

Beginner Program

WEEK	WARMUP	MILEAGE	PACE (mph)	HEART RATE (% of max.)	COOLDOWN	FREQUENCY (times per week)
1	5−7 mins. before-walk stretches	1.5	3.0	60−70	5−7 mins. after-walk stretches	5
2	5−7 mins.	1.5	3.0	60−70	5−7 mins.	5
3	5−7 mins.	1.75	3.0	60−70	5−7 mins.	5
4	5−7 mins.	1.75	3.0	60−70	5−7 mins.	5
5	5−7 mins.	2.0	3.0	60−70	5−7 mins.	5
6	5−7 mins.	2.0	3.0	60−70	5−7 mins.	5
7	5−7 mins.	2.0	3.5	70	5−7 mins.	5
8	5−7 mins.	2.25	3.5	70	5−7 mins.	5
9	5−7 mins.	2.25	3.5	70	5−7 mins.	5
10	5−7 mins.	2.5	3.5	70	5−7 mins.	5
11	5−7 mins.	2.5	3.5	70	5−7 mins.	5
12	5−7 mins.	2.55	3.5	70	5−7 mins.	5
13	5−7 mins.	2.75	3.5	70	5−7 mins.	5
14	5−7 mins.	2.75	4.0	70−80	5−7 mins.	5
15	5−7 mins.	3.0	4.0	70−80	5−7 mins.	5
16	5−7 mins.	3.0	4.0	70−80	5−7 mins.	5
17	5−7 mins.	3.25	4.0	70−80	5−7 mins.	5
18	5−7 mins.	3.25	4.0	70−80	5−7 mins.	5
19	5−7 mins.	3.5	4.0	70−80	5−7 mins.	5
20	5−7 mins.	3.5	4.0	70−80	5−7 mins.	5

At the end of the twenty-week fitness walking protocol you may either retest yourself and move to a new fitness walking category or turn to the Intermediate Maintenance Program for a lifetime of fitness walking.

Intermediate Program

If you scored in the "average" category on the step test or rated yourself in the "light physical activity" category on the self-rating scale, then the Intermediate Program is for you. Chances are you are already involved in some recreational activities or have completed either the Starter or the Beginner fitness walking protocol.

The Intermediate Program is designed to help you take the next step to a lifelong commitment to regular, vigorous exercise. Don't be surprised if you find your fitness walking program more strenuous than you had anticipated. Most of the Intermediate fitness walking protocols are at least as strenuous as vigorous singles tennis.

This is the time to make a true commitment to physical conditioning and strengthening your heart. Your Intermediate fitness walking protocol will get you started on a lifetime of health exercise.

Intermediate Program

WEEK	WARMUP	MILEAGE	PACE (mph)	HEART RATE (% of max.)	COOLDOWN	FREQUENCY (times per week)
1	5−7 mins. before-walk stretches	2.0	3.0	70	5−7 mins. after-walk stretches	5
2	5−7 mins.	2.25	3.0	70	5−7 mins.	5
3	5−7 mins.	2.5	3.0	70	5−7 mins.	5
4	5−7 mins.	2.5	3.0	70	5−7 mins.	5
5	5−7 mins.	2.75	3.0	70	5−7 mins.	5
6	5−7 mins.	2.75	3.5	70	5−7 mins.	5
7	5−7 mins.	2.75	3.5	70	5−7 mins.	5
8	5−7 mins.	2.75	3.5	70	5−7 mins.	5
9	5−7 mins.	3.0	3.5	70	5−7 mins.	5
10	5−7 mins.	3.0	3.5	70	5−7 mins.	5
11	5−7 mins.	3.0	4.0	70−80	5−7 mins.	5
12	5−7 mins.	3.0	4.0	70−80	5−7 mins.	5
13	5−7 mins.	3.25	4.0	70−80	5−7 mins.	5
14	5−7 mins.	3.25	4.0	70−80	5−7 mins.	5
15	5−7 mins.	3.5	4.0	70−80	5−7 mins.	5
16	5−7 mins.	3.5	4.5	70−80	5−7 mins.	5
17	5−7 mins.	3.5	4.5	70−80	5−7 mins.	5
18	5−7 mins.	4.0	4.5	70−80	5−7 mins.	5
19	5−7 mins.	4.0	4.5	70−80	5−7 mins.	5
20	5−7 mins.	4.0	4.5	70−80	5−7 mins.	5

At the end of the twenty-week fitness walking protocol you may either retest yourself and move to a new fitness walking category or turn to the Intermediate Maintenance Program for a lifetime of fitness walking.

Advanced Program

If you scored in the "good" category on the step test or rated yourself in the "moderate physical activity" category on the self-rating scale, then the Advanced Program is for you. If you are in this category, you have already made a commitment to regular exercise.

In the Advanced Program you begin with vigorous walking protocols and continue to some of the advanced techniques such as walking with weights or focusing on hill walking. In the last six weeks of the Advanced Program we recommend that you cut down to three sessions a week and supplement your fitness walking program with some light weight training or other forms of exercise.

As an advanced fitness walker you'll need to be concerned about the right equipment. Purchase a good pair of walking shoes designed for the serious walker (see Chapter 4) and an all-weather exercise suit. Focus on your technique and mental strategies to get the maximum benefit from the sport of fitness walking.

Advanced Program

WEEK	WARMUP	MILEAGE	PACE (mph)	INCLINE/ WEIGHT	HEART RATE (% of max.)	COOLDOWN	FREQUENCY (times per week)
1	5–7 mins. before- walk stretches	2.5	3.5		70	5–7 mins. after- walk stretches	5
2	5–7 mins.	2.75	3.5		70	5–7 mins.	5
3	5–7 mins.	3.0	3.5		70	5–7 mins.	5
4	5–7 mins.	3.0	3.5		70	5–7 mins.	5
5	5–7 mins.	3.25	3.5		70	5–7 mins.	5
6	5–7 mins.	3.25	4.0		70–80	5–7 mins.	5
7	5–7 mins.	3.5	4.0		70–80	5–7 mins.	5
8	5–7 mins.	3.75	4.0		70–80	5–7 mins.	5
9	5–7 mins.	4.0	4.0		70–80	5–7 mins.	5
10	5–7 mins.	4.0	4.0		70–80	5–7 mins.	5
11	5–7 mins.	4.0	4.5		70–80	5–7 mins.	5
12	5–7 mins.	4.0	4.5		70–80	5–7 mins.	5
13	5–7 mins.	4.0	4.5		70–80	5–7 mins.	5
14	5–7 mins.	4.0	4.5		70–80	5–7 mins.	5
15	5–7 mins.	4.0	4.5	+	70–80	5–7 mins.	3
16	5–7 mins.	4.0	4.5	+	70–80	5–7 mins.	3
17	5–7 mins.	4.0	4.5	+	70–80	5–7 mins.	3
18	5–7 mins.	4.0	4.5	+	70–80	5–7 mins.	3
19	5–7 mins.	4.0	4.5	+	70–80	5–7 mins.	3
20	5–7 mins.	4.0	4.5	+	70–80	5–7 mins.	3

At the end of the twenty-week fitness walking protocol turn to the Advanced/Expert Maintenance Program for a lifetime of fitness walking.

+ refers to weights (to upper body) or incline should be added as needed to keep heart rate in target zone (70 to 80 percent of the predicted maximum).

Expert Program

If you scored in the "excellent" category on the step test or rated yourself in the "very vigorous physical activity" category on the self-rating scale, then the Expert Program is for you. Congratulations! You have already made a serious commitment to regular exercise. You rate in the top 5 percent of fitness walkers in the United States.

Your goals should be to refine your technique and advance in the sport of fitness walking. Friends will ask you for advice, and you should help them develop their walking programs. As new equipment becomes available (such as advanced walking shoes), you should test it out and help advance the sport of fitness walking. Write to Rob at the Rockport Walking Institute, 72 Howe Street, Marlborough, Massachusetts 01752, and help him start a Fitness Walking Program in your community.

Expert Program

WEEK	WARMUP	MILEAGE	PACE (mph)	INCLINE/ WEIGHT	HEART RATE (% of max.)	COOLDOWN	FREQUENCY (times per week)
1	5–7 mins. before-walk stretches	3.0	4.0		70	5–7 mins. after-walk stretches	5
2	5–7 mins.	3.25				5–7 mins.	5
3	5–7 mins.	3.5				5–7 mins.	5
4	5–7 mins.	3.5	4.5		70--80	5–7 mins.	5
5	5–7 mins.	3.75	4.5		70–80	5–7 mins.	5
6	5–7 mins.	4.0	4.5		70–80	5–7 mins.	5
7	5–7 mins.	4.0	4.5	+	70–80	5–7 mins.	3
8	5–7 mins.		4.5	+	70–80	5–7 mins.	3
9	5–7 mins.		4.5	+	70–80	5–7 mins.	3
10	5–7 mins.		4.5	+	70–80	5–7 mins.	3
11	5–7 mins.		4.5	+	70–80	5–7 mins.	3
12	5–7 mins.		4.5	+	70–80	5–7 mins.	3
13	5–7 mins.		4.5	+	70–80	5–7 mins.	3
14	5–7 mins.		4.5	+	70–80	5–7 mins.	3
15	5–7 mins.		4.5	+	70–80	5–7 mins.	3
16	5–7 mins.		4.5	+	70–80	5–7 mins.	3
17	5–7 mins.		4.5	+	70–80	5–7 mins.	3
18	5–7 mins.		4.5	+	70–80	5–7 mins.	3
19	5–7 mins.		4.5	+	70–80	5–7 mins.	3
20	5–7 mins.		4.5	+	70–80	5–7 mins.	3

At the end of the twenty-week fitness walking protocol turn to the Advanced/Expert Maintenance Program for a lifetime of fitness walking.

+ refers to weights (to upper body) or incline should be added as needed to keep heart rate in target zone (70 to 80 percent of the predicted maximum).

Maintenance Programs

Congratulations!

When you've arrived at this section it means you've conscientiously applied yourself to at least twenty weeks of fitness walking. Or you are an experienced advanced or expert walker and want a maintenance program of fitness walking to add structure to your walking. In either case you've made a lifelong commitment to improved health through fitness walking.

The maintenance programs are designed to help you enjoy the benefits of a lifetime of fitness walking. The pointers in Chapter 4 will help you extend the benefits of fitness walking to a lifetime of improved total fitness. You should take the time to review these pointers periodically and think about the total picture.

Intermediate Maintenance Program

Total time: 1 hour

Warmup: 5 to 7 minutes of before-walk stretches

Aerobic workout: mileage: 4.0

                  pace: 4.5 miles per hour

Heart rate: 70 to 80 percent of maximum

Cooldown: 5 to 7 minutes of after-walk stretches

Frequency: 3 to 5 times per week

Weekly mileage: 12 to 15 miles

Advanced/Expert Maintenance Program

Total time: 1 hour

Warmup: 5 to 7 minutes of before-walk stretches

Aerobic workout: mileage: 4.0

                  pace: 4.5 miles per hour

                  weight/incline: weights (to upper body) or incline (hill walking) should be added as needed to keep heart rate in target zone (70 to 80 percent of the predicted maximum).

Heart rate: 70 to 80 percent of maximum

Cooldown: 5 to 7 minutes of after-walk exercises

Frequency: 3 times per week

Weekly mileage: 12 miles

CHAPTER 6

FOOD FOR
THE ROAD

The deeper and warmer the feeling of companionship during periods when I stayed with a family for a day or two, the tougher became my readjustment to the road.

On a Friday afternoon, with the sun setting behind the tall brown jagged rocks of Moses Coulee in Washington, I said good-bye to the Ruud and Rivers families of Waterville, Washington. John Ruud, the dogsled-racing dentist, had shown me the benefits of Bag Balm for weary feet. But now I was off, the sparsely inhabited farmlands of wintry central Washington state waiting, my next contact in Spokane, 100 miles away.

Little farm villages at ten- to 20-mile spreads would be my world of conversation for the next three days. The dropping mercury, the dying wind, the falling sun, the fading colors of the land all accentuated my mood. Nature had a way of telling me the party was over.

Walking circulated blood and prevented frostbite—the plumbers' answer to water-pipe freeze-up of the body. Darkness was almost complete when I came upon the weathered pine-wood shack leaning

◀ Rob with food and gear in waist packs.

askew as if undecided which way to fall. Through the tall weeds, I approached the abandoned structure, staring constantly through its busted windows to make sure some wild creature wasn't waiting there to lunge at me.

Inside the splintered shell, everything was gutted. Grass grew through the cracked concrete floor. In the crevices of rotted planks I searched until under a windowsill in the west wall, catching the glint of glass. John Ruud's son Jimmy had kept his word and stashed a bottle of apple juice. There was still gold in the mountains.

A cornerstone of our program is an understanding of how nutrition and weight control and fitness walking work together. What and how you eat and how you combine food with the right amount of exercise will help you achieve and maintain your desired body size.

Too much body fat is undesirable for a variety of reasons. First, obesity or "overfatness" is a risk factor for certain types of heart disease, high blood pressure, impaired carbohydrate and fat metabolism, joint, bone and gallbladder diseases, diabetes, asthma and some lung disorders. Being "too fat" is also often accompanied by changes in personality and behavior and can be marked by depression, withdrawal, self-pity, irritability and aggression.

Until recently, people believed that the major cause of obesity was simply overeating. That's not true. The underlying causes for excess caloric storage are many and complex. *One major cause is physical inactivity.*

It is truly remarkable that the body weight of most adults fluctuates only slightly during the year, even though the average annual intake of food fluctuates between 1600 and 1800 pounds! This stability is especially impressive when you consider that a very slight but *prolonged* increase in food intake can cause a substantial increase in body weight. Eating just an extra handful of peanuts each day would increase body weight by about ten pounds in one year.

The simplest statement of effective weight control is this: The only way to shed pounds is to expend more energy (calories) than you take in. That doesn't necessarily mean you have to eat less or entirely avoid fattening foods. The number of calories you burn up in exercise will help determine whether you gain weight or lose weight!

Many of the popular books that tout exotic diets or exercise programs fall into the common trap of claiming that their plan is so easy and effortless that results can be guaranteed. These flash-in-the-pan schemes to lose fat effortlessly simply do not work! If any of them did, there would be no clamor for new schemes from the 50 million men, 60 million women, and 10 million teenagers who need to shed excess fat.

One drawback to diet fads is that while they may produce a temporary reduction of body weight, they can also jeopardize the dieter's general health. This can be true with the high-fat or high-protein diets, which forbid necessary carbohydrates while permitting unlimited quantities of fats and proteins. This warning came from the American Medical Association Council on Food and Nutrition in response to inquiries about the Atkins high-fat "diet revolution": "Bizarre concepts of nutrition and dieting should not be promoted to the public as if they were established scientific principles. If appropriate precautions are not taken, information about nutrition and diet that is not only misleading but potentially dangerous to health will continue to be conveyed to the public." Similar warnings should be heeded for the so-called high-protein diets, which can place excessive strain on the liver and kidneys and could prove fatal to individuals predisposed to diseases of these vital organs.

Americans have extolled crackpot diets and fat-reducing schemes for over a century. One book even proclaims "Calories don't count." Some health food enthusiasts believe that all of man's ills can be cured by a diet featuring wheat germ, unrefined sugar, organic foods and lots of vitamin supplements.

"There is a lot of interest in nutrition," says nutrition expert Ken Samonds, director of the Department of Food, Science and Nutrition at the University of Massachusetts. "There's also a lot of misinformation. People believe nutrition does more than it can do." His department kept a record of every mouthful of food Rob swallowed on his 11,600-mile journey. The food was analyzed through the department's data bank, which contains the ingredients for 5000 different foods. "Most people are adequately nourished and don't have to add to or change their diets," Samonds says. "In fact, the people who are taking vitamin and mineral supplements are usually the people who don't need them. What people need is to exercise and, if they diet, they should do so by eating a little less of the things they eat. You can't eat a balanced diet and get the nutrients you need on one thousand calories a day."

We are concerned with the excesses proclaimed by faddists, and we do not believe that diet is the whole answer to fitness and health.

What Is the Best Diet?

The best diet may be defined as one in which the supply of required nutrients is enough for tissue maintenance, repair and growth. Within this framework, it would appear rather simple to establish recommendations for the appropriate intake of the various nutrients the body needs. That hasn't been the case, though. Only in the last few years has it been possible to obtain a reasonable estimate of the specific nutrient needs for men and women of different ages and body sizes, taking into consideration individual differences in digestion, storage capacity, metabolism and daily levels of activity.

Furthermore, diet recommendations for athletes, as well as others involved in exercise, may be complicated by the energy requirements of a certain sport, along with the athlete's dietary preferences. The general consensus of research is that athletes do *not* require additional nutrients beyond those obtained in a balanced diet. *In essence, sound nutrition for athletes is sound human nutrition.* The extra calories required for exercise can be obtained from a variety of foods.

The standard recommendation for protein intake is about 0.9 grams (or .032 ounces) of protein per kilogram (2.2 pounds) of body weight. A person who weighs 170 pounds (77.1 kilograms) would require about 69 grams, or 2.49 ounces, of protein daily. That amount is probably adequate for both active and sedentary persons. The average American diet significantly exceeds the recommended protein requirement, and the athlete's diet is usually two to three times in excess of the protein intake considered optimal.

The best sources of protein are eggs, milk, cheese and other dairy products as well as fish and meats. Vegetables are generally less complete sources of protein because they do not contain all the required amino acids in the proper proportions needed by the body. This does not mean that a vegetarian approach to nutrition is harmful. According to Samonds, Rob had no problem getting enough protein from his lacto-vegetarian diet of dairy products, vegetables and grains. Vegetarians who eat a varied diet, as Rob does, will meet their protein needs.

The amount of dietary fat varies widely according to personal taste, money spent on food, and the availability of fat-rich foods. For example, people living in Asia receive only about 10 percent of their energy from fats in their diet. In the United States, Canada, Scandinavia, Germany and France, fat accounts for 40 to 45 percent of the caloric intake.

For best health, fat intake should not exceed more than 30 percent of the energy content of one's diet. An optimal diet would strive for 20 percent. Of this, at least half should be in the form of unsaturated fats, which are generally fats of vegetable origin. Research indicates that individuals with diets high in saturated fat tend to be more susceptible to coronary heart disease, as well as other diseases such as cancer and diabetes. However, eliminating all fat from the diet restricts the amount of carbohydrate, protein, essential fatty acids and vitamins A, D, E and K entering the body, eventually resulting in a relative state of malnutrition.

Carbohydrate-rich foods such as grains, starchy roots, dried peas and beans are usually the cheapest foods in relation to their energy value. In the Far East, carbohydrates (rice) contribute 80 percent of the total caloric intake, while in the United States only about 40 to 50 percent of the energy requirement comes from carbohydrates. For a physically active person, *the sensible diet should contain at least 50 to 60 percent of its calories in the form of carbohydrates.*

The Four Food Group Plan:
The Essentials of Adequate Nutrition

A practical approach to sound nutrition is unfortunately neither new nor chic. Simply choose foods from each category in the Four Food Group Plan illustrated in Table 2. As long as you eat the recommended number of daily servings from each group, you will receive adequate nutrition.

Table 3 shows three daily menus formulated from the guidelines. Each menu provides all the essential nutrients, even though the energy value of each is considerably below the average adult requirement. These menus serve as excellent nutritional models for reducing diets.

The Weight-Loss Secret

The secret formula to lose weight and fat: Restrict your calories while exercising enough to burn up body fat. While you are cutting down your calories, make sure to eat a well-balanced diet to get proper nutrition.

Generally limit your weight loss to a pound or two a week. We recommend this because individuals who have successfully achieved and *maintained* a desirable body weight lost no more than 1.5 pounds per week.

Proteins, carbohydrates and fats are all essential. In fact, about 12 to 15 percent of your calories should come from protein, 20 to 30 percent from fat, and the remainder from carbohydrates, preferably as starches. And while you're at it, throw away your vitamin supplements unless they've been recommended by your physician. Forget the gimmicks, schemes and potions. If you follow a common-sense diet and exercise regimen, you will lose weight, your fat will diminish and your physical well-being should improve considerably.

Table 2. The Four Food Group Plan (the foundation of a good diet).

Category	Examples	Recommended Daily Servings
1. Milk and milk products[a]	Milk, cheese, ice cream, sour cream, yogurt	2
2. Meat and high-protein[b] foods	Meat,[c] fish, poultry, eggs (dried beans, peas, nuts, or peanut butter are alternatives)	2
3. Vegetables and fruits[d]	Dark green or yellow vegetables; citrus fruits or tomatoes	4
4. Cereal and grain food	Enriched breads, cereals, flour, baked goods, or whole-grain products	4

[a] If large quantities of milk are normally consumed, *fortified* skimmed milk should be substituted to reduce the quantity of saturated fats.

[b] Fish, chicken, and high-protein vegetables contain significantly less saturated fat than other protein sources.

[c] The basic serving of meat or fish is usually 100 grams, or 3.5 ounces, of edible food.

[d] To preserve the vitamin and mineral content of vegetables, stew them or eat them uncooked.

Table 3. Three daily menus formulated from guidelines established by the Four Food Group Plan. Each menu provides all essential nutrients; the energy or caloric value of the diet can be easily increased by increasing the size of the portions, the frequency of meals, or the variety of foods consumed at one sitting.

3 Meals a Day

Breakfast
½ cup unsweetened grapefruit juice
1 poached egg
1 slice toast
1 teaspoon butter or margarine
½ cup skim milk
tea or coffee, black

Lunch
2 ounces lean roast beef
½ cup cooked summer squash
1 slice rye bread
1 teaspoon butter or margarine
1 cup skim milk
10 grapes

Dinner
3 ounces poached haddock
½ cup cooked spinach
tomato-and-lettuce salad
1 teaspoon oil; vinegar or lemon
1 small biscuit
1 teaspoon butter or margarine
½ cup canned drained fruit cocktail
½ cup skim milk

5 Meals a Day

Breakfast
½ grapefruit
⅔ cup bran flakes
1 cup skim or low-fat milk or other beverage

Snack
1 small package raisins
½ bologna sandwich

Lunch
1 slice pizza
carrot sticks
1 apple
1 cup skim or low-fat milk

Snack
1 banana

Dinner
baked fish with mushrooms (3 oz.)
baked potato
2 teaspoons margarine
½ cup broccoli
1 cup tomato juice or skim or low-fat milk

6 Small Meals a Day

Breakfast
½ cup orange juice
¾ cup ready-to-eat cereal
½ cup skim milk
tea or coffee, black

Mid-morning Snack
⅓ cup low-fat cottage cheese

Lunch
2 ounces sliced turkey on 1 slice white toast
1 teaspoon butter or margarine
2 canned drained peach halves
½ cup skim milk

Mid-afternoon Snack
1 cup fresh spinach-and-lettuce salad
2 teaspoons oil; vinegar or lemon
3 saltines

Dinner
1 cup clear broth
3 ounces broiled chicken breast
⅓ cup cooked rice with 1 teaspoon butter or margarine
¼ cup cooked mushrooms
½ cup cooked broccoli
½ cup skim milk

Evening Snack
1 medium apple
½ cup skim milk

Total Calories:
about 1200

Total Calories:
about 1400

Total Calories:
about 1200

The Energy Balance Equation

Excess fat is the result of an imbalance in the "energy balance equation," which states that for your weight to remain constant, you have to use as many calories as you take in. An accumulation of 3500 "extra" calories due to an imbalance on either side of the equation is equal to about one pound of stored fat.

For example, eating an extra apple (70 calories) each day and keeping your energy output the same increases your yearly caloric intake by the amount equivalent to about seven pounds of body fat. An additional slice of cherry, apple or mince pie daily would cause about 35 pounds of excess fat to accumulate in a year.

On the other hand, to lose one pound you must create an energy deficit of 3500 calories, either by cutting your energy intake (dieting) or by increasing your energy output (exercise). If your daily food intake is reduced by only 100 calories and your energy expenditure increased by 100 calories by walking at a brisk pace for 20 minutes, the monthly caloric deficit will amount to 6000 calories—a weight loss of 1.75 pounds. That's 21 pounds in a year.

Unbalancing the Equation

There are three ways to tip the energy balance equation in your favor to reduce fat and weight.

1. Reduce calories taken in from food and drink *below* daily energy expenditure (dieting).

2. Maintain your regular food intake level but *increase* your caloric output by stepping up physical activity so that it exceeds your daily energy requirements (exercising).

3. Combine both these methods by *decreasing* food consumption and *increasing* energy expenditure (diet and exercise).

Suppose an obese woman who consumes 2800 calories daily and weighs 175 pounds wishes to lose weight. She maintains her regular level of activity but reduces her daily food intake to 1800 calories to create a 1000-calorie deficit. In seven days the caloric deficit would equal 7000 calories, the equivalent of two pounds of body fat. Actually, considerably more than two pounds would be lost during the first week because the body's carbohydrate stores would be used up first. This stored nutrient contains fewer calories and much more water than fat. This is why short periods of dieting often prove encouraging but result in a large percentage of water and carbohydrate loss with only a minimal decrease in body fat. Then, as weight loss continues, a larger proportion of fat is used for energy to supply the deficit created by food restriction.

To reduce fat by another three pounds, the reduced intake of 1800 calories would have to be maintained for another 10.5 days. If the woman held to this diet, she could theoretically lose one pound every 3.5 days. In practice, though, other factors enter in.

Dieting frequently causes lethargy and reduces one's daily activity level. In addition, as weight decreases, the energy cost of moving the body is reduced. Consequently, the energy output side of the "energy balance equation" becomes smaller. Also, physiological changes may occur during dieting that can affect the rate at which weight loss occurs. One such change is the resting metabolic rate, which declines with semi-starvation. It actually conserves energy and causes the diet to be less effective. This "slowing up" of weight loss often leaves the dieter frustrated and discouraged.

If the diet is nutritionally sound, what you eat matters less than how many calories you consume. Weight loss will occur with a reduced caloric intake regardless of the diet's percentages of carbohydrate, protein and fat. With obese patients who consumed either an 800-calorie high-fat diet or an 800-calorie high-carbohydrate diet, the weight loss on each diet was nearly identical, as was the percentage of fat tissue lost over the ten-day period.

Anyone contemplating a diet that deviates from a low-calorie but well-balanced one should consult a physician. Adequate water intake should be maintained at all times during dieting. While restricting water intake will result in a relatively large initial weight loss, this is substantially due to a loss in body water.

For men and women, combinations of exercise and diet offer considerably more flexibility for losing weight than either exercise or diet alone. Even more important, the addition of exercise to the diet program may help make the weight loss permanent.

To lose one pound a week (a sensible goal), the average weekly deficit would have to be 3500 calories (a daily deficit of 500 calories). A half hour of moderate exercise (about 350 "extra" calories) performed three days a week gives 1050 calories on the deficit side. Therefore, the weekly food intake would have to be reduced by only 2450 calories instead of 3500. If the exercise is increased from three to five days, food intake would only have to be reduced by 250 calories each day. If the exercise was an hour instead of 30 minutes, five days a week, then you wouldn't have to cut food intake at all because the required 3500-calorie deficit would be achieved through exercise alone.

Clearly, physical activity is effective by itself or in combination with mild dietary restriction to give you an effective loss of body fat. This approach also is likely to produce fewer feelings of intense hunger and other psychological stresses that occur with a program of weight loss that relies on dieting alone.

If your purpose is to reduce excess fat and at the same time get your cardiovascular system in shape without losing lean tissue, the best procedure is to *reduce* calories and *increase* exercise. Dieting alone is almost always doomed to failure. Rapidly lost weight is easily regained, but lean tissue is hard to rebuild.

A Final Word on Calories

The word "calorie" has tremendous significance to millions of people. The reason is probably fear of fat—gaining it and not being able to get rid of it. For most people who are concerned about their weight, the words "calorie" and "fat" are inseparable, if not interchangeable.

The energy value of foods is measured in calories. By scientific definition, a calorie is a precise measure of heat: It is the amount of heat necessary to raise the temperature of one milliliter of water one degree centigrade. In general, high-calorie foods have a high energy content and low-calorie foods have a low energy content.

A very small serving of some foods can have the same caloric value as very large quantities of other foods. You would need to consume more than 400 stalks of celery or 80 cups of cabbage to supply the daily energy needs of a fairly sedentary person, while this same energy could be supplied by eating only 20 tablespoons of mayonnaise or about seven and one-half ounces of salad oil. There is no difference between calories from an energy standpoint.

It's important to remember that the calories consumed in food are cumulative. There is no getting around it—the more calories you consume, the more energy you store. If the food you eat has a high concentration of calories, as in fatty foods, and you take even a small portion, you consume a relatively high number of calories.

Nutrition Throughout Life

As individuals age, their nutritional needs change. Here are some basic guidelines on changing calorie needs.

Nutrition in infancy. The normal infant requires about 50 calories per pound of body weight per day. This should consist of a high protein intake because of rapid growth rate, as well as small amounts of fat to provide essential fatty acids, and a relatively high fluid intake.

Nutrition in childhood and adolescence. Growth is a gradual process, but it accelerates dramatically during puberty. The average caloric intake for teenage boys eleven to fourteen years is 2800 calories, and 3000 calories from ages fifteen to eighteen. For girls, the level of caloric intake remains at 2400 calories throughout adolescence, more than at any other time of their life with the exception of pregnancy.

Nutrition for adults. The mature adult, depending on occupation and other physical activity, needs fewer calories to maintain weight, from 1600 to 2100, depending on body size. The proportion of protein and carbohydrate in the diet should be the same as in adolescence with a lower fat percent.

Geriatric nutrition. Proper nutrition for the person over age sixty is similar to normal nutrition in the mature adult. As individuals age, their basal metabolic rate decreases and fewer calories are needed to meet energy requirements. If food consumption is decreased substantially to combat overweight, or for other reasons, poor choices of food may result in protein or vitamin deficiency.

139

Nutrition Tips for Fitness Walkers

Nutrition for Optimum Performance

Individuals often experience "staleness" or unusual fatigue when training. This is related to the gradual depletion of the body's carbohydrate reserves. Thus, maintaining an adequate level of carbohydrate in the muscles is important for optimal exercise performance. Carbohydrate intake is also desirable because it enhances the utilization of fat as an energy source during exercise.

Of the various nutrients we eat, carbohydrates and fats, and to a lesser extent proteins, provide the main source of energy for muscular work. Carbohydrates—such as pasta, potatoes, bread, beans, fruits and vegetables—are digested and absorbed more rapidly than either protein or fats. This makes it more readily available as an energy source and may also reduce the feeling of fullness usually experienced after eating. Equally important for favoring a higher than normal carbohydrate intake in training is that carbohydrates are the main nutrient energy source for intense as well as more prolonged activity.

Cooking for Good Health

Cooking for good health does not mean discarding favorite recipes and cookbooks. You can continue to enjoy your favorite foods by substituting some ingredients and making slight changes in cooking methods. This will help reduce fat intake and calorie consumption. Here are some basic tips for more healthful eating.

O When the recipe says "fry" or "sauté," try broiling, poaching or steaming instead.

- Use a good nonstick skillet. This avoids the need for fats in frying and sautéing.
- Use nonstick sprays and coatings for fat-free frying, sautéing, and when greasing pans for baking.
- Strip meat of all visible fat and remove the skin from chicken prior to cooking.
- Brown meat in a nonstick skillet without fat, or under the broiler so that the fat drips off.
- Avoid browning vegetables with meat. Vegetables soak fat up and increase fat intake.
- Drain fat from browned ground beef by using a colander or paper towels.
- Refrigerate soups, stews, meat drippings and sauces. The hardened fat surface can then be removed before rewarming.
- Tenderize leaner cuts of meat by soaking them in a fat-free marinade.

Nutrition and the Energy Value of Foods

The three main food nutrients, carbohydrates, fats and proteins, provide nearly all the energy required by the body on a daily basis. The heat liberated by the burning or oxidation of the food is referred to as its heat of combustion. This represents the total energy value (kcal) of the particular food nutrient.

Fat liberates 65 percent more energy per gram than protein, and 120 percent more energy than an equal amount of carbohydrate. Thus, foods high in fat content contain more kcal than equal amounts of foods that are fat free. For example, one cup of whole milk contains 160 kcal, whereas the same quantity of skim milk contains 90 kcal. If someone who normally consumes one quart of whole milk each day were to switch to skim milk, the total kcal ingest each year would be reduced by an amount equal to 25 pounds of fat.

By knowing the approximate kcal value of foods, it is possible to reconstruct the total energy intake for an individual over a specified time period.

Energy Expenditure

Levels of energy expenditure range from the truly sedentary person who rarely does anything more strenuous than walking slowly around the house to lumberjacks and athletes who may perform vigorous physical activities six to eight hours a day.

According to numerous surveys, about one-third of a person's time is spent resting. In total, about three-fourths of the average man's and woman's working day is spent in sedentary activities. This predominance of physical inactivity has prompted some to refer to the modern-day American as *Homo sedentarius*. It is probably a fair estimate that only about 50 percent of adult American men and women engage in physical activities that require an energy expenditure much above the resting level.

Several systems have been proposed for rating the difficulty of work in terms of intensity. The system we use classifies work into categories designated as light, moderate, heavy, very heavy and extremely heavy. Intensity is expressed in terms of energy production per unit of time.

Average Time Spent During the Day by Men and Women

ACTIVITY	TIME IN HOURS
Sleeping and resting	8
Sitting	6
Standing	6
Walking	2
Recreational sports or exercise	2

Classification of Physical Work in Terms of Intensity

WORK INTENSITY	ENERGY EXPENDITURE, Kcal min.	
	MEN	WOMEN
Light	2.3–5.3	1.5–3.6
Moderate	5.3–8.1	3.6–5.6
Heavy	8.1–10.7	5.6–7.7
Very Heavy	10.7–13.4	7.7–9.8
Extremely Heavy	Above 13.4	Above 9.8

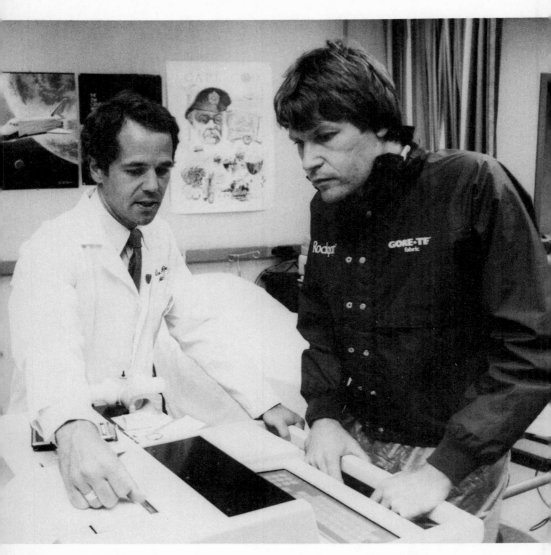

Rob confers with Dr. James Rippe during a series of tests conducted prior to beginning his 11,600-mile walk. Photo by Chuck Kidd.

CHAPTER 7

FITNESS WALKING
FOR CARDIAC
REHABILITATION

Inspiration came from a lot of places: the smile on the face of the little farmer boy in the back of the truck, the people who waved as they drove by, the people who took time.

Bradenton, Florida. In front of me sat sixteen alcoholics on a variety of chairs and couches that looked as worn as the men's faces. Gray beards, flushed red faces with scars, half-shut eyes, a few quivering hands, thin and fat bodies. A United Nations of taverners. I thought those sixteen could tell tales of hardship and disease for days on end, but it was my turn to speak.

The slides flashed of places I had been. I talked about life on the road, food, blisters, a map of the tour. They were interested. For them, it must have seemed like a science fiction thriller. How will that man cross the Arizona desert and walk over the snow-covered mountains? Will his feet dissolve in the Pacific rain? Will boredom kill him in Texas?

FITNESS WALKING

They asked the same questions everyone else asks while I talked about the heart, blood vessels, fatty deposits, smoking's effect on the blood vessels, reducing high blood pressure, controlling weight, good exercise programs. With the last slide, "Today is the first day of the rest of your life," came a round of applause. Good questions about diet, exercise, alcohol and the heart.

One more question. A thin, gray-haired unshaven man stuttered as if the words were too big to spit out.

"You know, Rob, I see something very similar in what you and all of us here need to do."

"What's that?" I asked unknowingly.

"All of us, including you, have to take life one day at a time."

He had said it all.

The principles of fitness walking are ideally suited for cardiac rehabilitation. We treat over six hundred new cardiac rehabilitation patients each year—and every one of them is given a walking program!

Walking is both the most flexible and most physiologic form of exercise. We're able to start patients on a very gentle walking program within four days of a heart attack and often within two days of open heart surgery! Patients love it. Walking gets them out of bed, feeling optimistic and feeling like they're taking charge of their lives. If you or a family member or friend has suffered a heart attack, has angina or has undergone open heart surgery, a fitness walking program for cardiac rehabilitation may be just right for you.

A word of caution. Cardiac rehabilitation is a serious business. In this chapter we give you all the information and tools you will need to start on a fitness walking program for cardiac rehabilitation. We *don't,* however, recommend that you try to do it alone. Any individual with serious heart disease should be under a physician's care.

If you want to use the fitness walking program as the basis of your cardiac rehabilitation program, we recommend that you take this book with you the next time you go in for a checkup. Show your doctor the walking protocols at the end of this chapter and discuss how they apply to your situation. We bet you'll find your doctor is happy to start you on a fitness walking program.

The Scope of the Problem

Each year, over a million Americans suffer heart attacks. More than half of these individuals die before they reach the hospital. Of the 500,000 who survive, the majority will suffer some degree of long-term disability.

Think about it for a moment: More than 300,000 people each year suffer some long-term problem as a result of a heart attack. It's a great personal tragedy for each of them and a terrible waste to society. It's exactly this group of people that cardiac rehabilitation can help.

Comprehensive Cardiac Rehabilitation

In this chapter we focus primarily on how fitness walking can serve as a cornerstone of cardiac rehabilitation. But cardiac rehabilitation involves much more than just exercise. *Comprehensive* cardiac rehabilitation programs achieve the better results.

Comprehensive programs take care of all of the needs of the patient, and address all of his or her concerns. A person who suffers a heart attack confronts many questions and anxieties. The cardiac rehabilitation program should help patients deal with psychological issues, provide specific information to help the patient reduce risk factors and know when it's safe to return to work (and what modifications of work may be necessary) and help both the patient and family members understand the heart attack and what to expect. Cardiac rehabilitation doesn't take the place of your physician's advice. Rather, it supplements his or her efforts. Here are a couple of points that we feel are particularly important.

1. *Risk factor reduction.* The same risk factors that increase your chance of having a first heart attack also increase your chance of having a second one. Cigarette smoking, elevated blood cholesterol and high blood pressure place the cardiac rehabilitation patient under unacceptably high risk for having a second heart attack. For example, one study showed that individuals who continued smoking cigarettes following a heart attack exposed themselves to twice the risk of a heart attack within the next two years compared with individuals who stopped.

2. *Resumption of normal activities.* Individuals who have had a heart attack wonder when they can resume normal activities. While some individual differences do exist, we typically allow an individual to drive a car two or three weeks following the heart attack and climb stairs and resume sexual intercourse two weeks following the heart attack as long as they are not having any worrisome symptoms such as chest pain or shortness of breath.

3. *Psychological recovery.* The psychological recovery from a heart attack is very important. The individual and his or her family must understand that some degree of anxiety and depression is common following a heart attack. Support and understanding will go a long way toward helping the individual recover.

Phases of Cardiac Rehabilitation

The best way to think about cardiac rehabilitation is to divide the process into phases. Each phase builds on the previous one. We like to divide the cardiac rehabilitation process into four phases.

Phase I begins in the coronary care unit and lasts throughout the time that the patient is in the hospital. We always obtain a low-level (modified) exercise test on the treadmill prior to discharging the individual from the hospital. This test tells us whether or not it is safe for the individual to go home and also gives us the information we need to make the right walking prescription.

Phase II is an outpatient program that lasts from six to ten weeks, depending on the individual needs of the patient. During this time we like to have the individual participate in a daily, low-intensity walking program. At this stage the goal is not to start conditioning but to get the muscles used to activity again. At the end of eight to ten weeks, we have the individual undergo a full exercise test on the treadmill. If the results of this test are satisfactory, we allow the individual to return to work and start a fitness walking program to improve cardiovascular fitness.

Phase III is the conditioning phase of the cardiac rehabilitation program. During this phase, the patient tries to improve his or her level of conditioning and cardiac function through a program of fitness walking. The goal is similar to that of any individual in a fitness walking program. The only difference is that the patient progresses a little slower in order to ensure safety while pursuing fitness goals.

Can individuals who have suffered a heart attack achieve the same levels of fitness as other individuals? The answer is a qualified *yes.* Your overall aerobic fitness level reflects both the ability of the heart to pump oxygenated blood to the muscles and their ability to pull oxygen from the blood. Even if you have suffered damage to your heart, you can still improve its function. And tremendous improvement in the efficiency of the muscles can occur with fitness walking. Many of our cardiac rehabilitation patients report that they are in the best shape of their lives following a few months of progressive walking protocols. When we measure their fitness levels, we find dramatic improvement.

Phase IV is the final stage of cardiac rehabilitation. This is the lifelong maintenance program. During this phase the individual consolidates the gains made in Phase III and adopts a lifelong program of fitness walking and risk factor reduction. As we've said, walking is the perfect exercise for a lifelong fitness program. This is particularly true for the individual who has angina, has had a heart attack or has undergone open heart surgery.

Fitness Walking Principles for Cardiac Rehabilitation

Many of the principles of fitness walking discussed elsewhere in this book apply equally well to individuals who wish to use the program for cardiac rehabilitation. Purchasing the right equipment (particularly shoes) is very important, and you should refer to Chapter 4 for advice. There are some important principles, however, which apply specifically to fitness walking for cardiac rehabilitation.

1. *See your physician* before starting your fitness walking program. This bears repeating. View your cardiac rehabilitation program as a partnership with your physician. Take this book in with you on your next office visit, show your physician the fitness walking protocol you have selected and get his or her permission to proceed.

2. *Listen to your body.* A symptom that worries you during your walking program usually indicates that your body is trying to tell you something. If you have chest pain, excessive shortness of breath or palpitations, you should stop walking and wait for the symptoms to go away or take nitroglycerin. If your symptoms don't go away rapidly, call your doctor or go to the nearest hospital. Even if your symptoms go away promptly, it's still important to call your doctor and discuss the situation. Perhaps a minor adjustment in your medication will resolve the problem.

3. *Long, Slow Distance* (LSD). Experienced long-distance walkers such as Rob know the important conditioning value of long distances covered at a moderate pace. This principle is particularly important when you are fitness walking for cardiac rehabilitation. When you look at the fitness walking protocols for cardiac rehabilitation, you'll notice several important differences from the rest of the fitness walking protocols. First of all, both the warmup and cooldown periods are quite long. These periods are particularly important for safety in cardiac rehabilitation. Second, we favor progressively longer periods of exercise at each level, rather than increased intensity.

4. *Risk factor reduction.* Although we hope that all people who start fitness walking programs will try to lower their risk factors, it is so important for cardiac rehabilitation patients that we list it as a separate component of the exercise prescription.

 # Protocols for Cardiac Rehabilitation

The specific fitness walking protocols for Phases II, III, and IV are listed here. There is no protocol for Phase I since Phase I occurs while the individual is still hospitalized.

Fitness Walking for Cardiac Rehabilitation

Phase II: Fitness Walking Immediately Following Hospital Discharge[a]

WEEK	WARMUP	PACE (mph)	HEART RATE (beats per min.)	DURATION (mins.)	COOLDOWN	FREQUENCY (times per week)	OTHER
1	10–15 mins. be-fore-walk stretches[b]	1.5	RHR + 10[c]	15	15 mins. after-walk stretches[b]	5	education / risk factor reduction[d]
2	"	2.0	"	20	"	"	"
3	"	2.0	"	30	"	"	"
4	"	2.0	RHR + 15	40	"	"	"
5	"	2.0	"	50	"	"	"
6	"	2.0	"	60	"	"	"
7	"	2.5	RHR + 20	40	"	"	"
8[e]	"	2.5	"	45	"	"	"
9	"	2.5	"	50	"	"	"
10	"	2.5	"	60	"	"	"

[a]Fitness walking for cardiac rehabilitation should not be undertaken without the consent of your personal physician.

[b]See pages 97–104 for recommended sequence of before- and after-walking stretches.

[c]RHR means "resting heart rate." Measure your heart rate at rest, then exercise at the prescribed heart rate as indicated. (See page 114 for the proper technique of pulse taking.)

[d]Education about heart disease and risk factor reduction are important components of cardiac rehabilitation. See pages 155–56.

[e]At Week 8 we recommend an exercise test on the treadmill supervised by your physician.

FITNESS WALKING

Phase III: Fitness Walking Conditioning Program from 8 weeks to 5 Months Following Hospitalization[a]

WEEK	WARMUP	PACE (mph)	HEART RATE[c] (beats per min.)	DURATION (mins.)	COOLDOWN	FREQUENCY (times per week)	OTHER
1	10–15 mins. be-fore-walk stretches[b]	3.0	60	40	15 mins. after-walk stretches[b]	5	education/ risk factor reduction[d]
2	"	3.0	60	40	"	"	"
3	"	3.0	60	50	"	"	"
4	"	3.0	60	50	"	"	"
5	"	3.0	60	60	"	"	"
6	"	3.0	60	60	"	"	"
7	"	3.5	60–70	40	"	"	"
8	"	3.5	60–70	40	"	"	"
9	"	3.5	60–70	50	"	"	"
10	"	3.5	60–70	50	"	"	"
11	"	3.5	60–70	60	"	"	"
12	"	4.0	70–75	60	"	"	"
13	"	4.0	70–75	40	"	"	"
14	"	4.0	70–75	40	"	"	"
15	"	4.0	70–75	50	"	"	"
16	"	4.0	70–75	50	"	"	"
17	"	4.0	70–75	60	"	"	"
18	"	4.0	70–75	60	"	"	"
19	"	4.0	70–75	60	"	"	"
20[e]	"	4.0	70–75	60	"	"	"

[a]Fitness walking for cardiac rehabilitation should not be undertaken without the consent of your personal physician. The conditioning program outlined here assumes you have undergone a physician-supervised treadmill exercise test before starting.

[b]See pages 97–104 for recommended sequence of before- and after-walking stretches.

[c]Maximum heart rate is determined on the treadmill exercise test. The proper technique for pulse taking is described on page 114.

[d]Education about heart disease and risk factor reduction are important components of cardiac re-habilitation.

[e]After twenty weeks, *if your physician agrees,* you can begin the lifelong cardiac rehabilitation mainte-nance program or take the tests on pages 66–70 and use the regular fitness walking protocols.

Fitness Walking for Cardiac Rehabilitation

Fitness Walking for Cardiac Rehabilitation
*Lifelong Fitness Walking Maintenance Protocol**

Warmup: 10 to 15 minutes before-walk stretches. (See pages 97–104 for recommended sequence of before-walking stretches.)

Aerobic workout: duration: 60 minutes
                              pace: 4.0 miles per hour

Heart rate: 70 to 80 percent of maximum. (The proper technique for taking pulse and determining maximum heart rate is described on page 114.)

Cooldown: 10 to 15 minutes after-walk stretches. (See pages 97–104 for recommended sequence of after-walk stretches.)

Frequency: 3 to 5 times per week

Other: Risk factor reduction. (Lifelong risk factor reduction is an important part of cardiac rehabilitation. Pointers on risk factor reduction are found on pages 155–56 and elsewhere in this book.)

Weekly Mileage: 12 to 20 miles

*Fitness walking for cardiac rehabilitation should not be undertaken without the consent of your physician. The lifelong maintenance program assumes that you are at least five months away from your heart attack or open heart surgery and have completed the Phase II and Phase III programs.

CHAPTER 8

WALKING AND TOTAL FITNESS

A walking program is the foundation for total fitness, but other important factors must be given serious consideration and emphasis. These "other factors" include nutrition, risk factor reduction, flexibility, lifestyle and strength, all of which have been discussed in this book. However, it is essential to reinforce them in perspective with your total well-being. After highlighting these factors, we will conclude by stressing the ongoing values of fitness walking and aerobic conditioning in order to leave a lasting impression.

Proper nutrition is of such great importance to your total fitness that we devoted all of Chapter 6 to the subject. It almost is redundant and simplistic to say that you should eat a well-balanced diet, yet it must be included here. Of the various nutrients, carbohydrates are of particular importance to fitness walkers.

Just as we can control our diet, we can control most of the risk factors for the development of coronary heart disease (CHD). These risk factors, based on the Framingham Study and several other studies, include the following:

◀ *Rob leaving Janesville, Wisconsin, as he heads for Brooklyn, Wisconsin, on one of the many country roads he traveled.* Photo by *Janesville Gazette.*

FITNESS WALKING

Major Risk Factors

1. Cigarette Smoking
2. Elevated Cholesterol
3. High Blood Pressure

Minor Risk Factors

1. Obesity
2. Family History of CHD
3. Sedentary Lifestyle
4. Diabetes
5. Stress

Rob Sweetgall is living proof and a prime example of how almost every risk factor can be reduced.

Another key element in any total fitness program concerns your ability to maintain or increase flexibility. Flexibility is covered in Chapter 4, which details why stretching exercises should be performed *before* and *after* each session of fitness walking.

Lifestyle is another area where fitness walking can be very helpful. Even if you have many things to accomplish in a day, you can exercise and experience the sense of refreshment you get by having some time to yourself. The ability to clear your thoughts will help you put things in perspective. If you exercise on a regular basis, you'll find that you spend much more time actually concentrating and less time "spinning your wheels." In extreme cases of "uptight" individuals, fitness walking can be an even more beneficial activity. Not only does it provide excellent exercise, it also helps relieve the personality traits that may be exposing those individuals to an increased risk of coronary heart disease.

If you decide to supplement your walking program with weight training, it is time for a few words of caution. Weight training, perhaps more than any other form of exercise, requires careful attention to safety precautions in order to avoid injuries. If you have any questions about the safety of weight training, talk with your doctor and an exercise specialist. This is especially true for males past the age of thirty-five and females past forty.

Unlike weight training for strength, fitness walking is safe and epitomizes the multiple benefits of aerobic conditioning. The word "aerobics" was popularized by Dr. Ken Cooper of Dallas in the late 1960s. However, the concept of aerobic exercise has existed for about fifty years. Today, "aerobics" is used in a variety of contexts. Millions of Americans are involved in "aerobic" dance, people are encouraged to perform "aerobic" exercise, and even casual athletes are concerned about "aerobic" conditioning. But what exactly is aerobic conditioning?

On the most fundamental level, aerobic means "in the presence of oxygen." In order for your muscles and body organs to work, they must produce and use energy. Under maximum exercise conditions, a given muscle group may require as much as twenty times the energy supply that it uses at rest! To produce this energy, the body must have two things: a source of fuel to burn and a way to burn it. The source of fuel initially comes from the food we eat. The fuel is then burned by the body in the presence of oxygen (aerobic metabolism) or in the absence of oxygen (anaerobic metabolism).

Anyone who is familiar with building a fire will understand why the body prefers to burn fuel in the presence of oxygen. With plenty of oxygen available, a fire burns with great intensity and heat. However, if you shut off or limit the oxygen supply, the fire smolders. It produces a lot of smoke, but burns much less efficiently. A very similar process occurs in the body. The muscles prefer to burn fuel in the presence of oxygen (aerobically).

Your body delivers both the fuel and the oxygen through the bloodstream. When you exercise, the muscles begin to call for more fuel and oxygen and your body responds in two ways. First, the amount of blood that the heart pumps out is dramatically increased. During maximum exertion the amount pumped out in a minute may be six or seven times the amount pumped at rest! Second, the muscles become much more efficient at extracting oxygen from the red blood cells.

The kinds of exercise that are most healthy for your heart are those that improve your aerobic capacity. As you become better conditioned, your heart becomes more efficient at delivering oxygen and your muscles become better able to use it. The combination of changes that occur as you get into better shape are called "training effects." The important point to keep in mind is that the way to improve your aerobic condition is to put moderate, consistent stress on the system. This is best done by performing exercises that use large muscle groups in a repetitive fashion.

People often wonder about the aerobic benefits of fitness walking. Sure, they say, fitness walking leads to fewer injuries and may be safer, but I'll bet I get more aerobic benefit from jogging. Well, they both work. The point is to get your heart rate up into the target zone for a duration of 20 to 30 minutes, and you can accomplish this easily with fitness walking.

FITNESS WALKING

What about the potential for weight loss? Did you know that you burn just as many calories walking a mile as you do jogging one? Thus, walking holds great promise as a means of calorie output.

How does fitness walking stack up against other common activities? Even at low to moderate levels, fitness walking can burn as many calories as recreational cycling or dancing. Once you get into the more advanced fitness walking routines, the comparison with other sports becomes dramatic. A glance at Figure 2 will show you what we mean. Even an intermediate program, such as moderate walking (3.5 mph) up a mild, five percent incline, burns more calories per minute than either fast cycling or vigorous singles tennis. If you reach an advanced program, such as brisk walking (4.0 mph) up a moderate, 10 percent incline, you burn as many calories in 25 minutes as you would if you played vigorous singles tennis for 43 minutes, cycled rapidly for 42 minutes or did recreational cycling for more than an hour.

Figure 2 shows you how many minutes are required in a variety of activities for a 150-pound male to burn 300 calories. The figure of 300 calories was not chosen at random. A number of studies have shown that workouts that burn this number of calories are excellent for achieving cardiovascular fitness.

What does it mean to burn 300 calories in a workout? An average-sized male who weighs 150 pounds and expends 300 extra calories a day for a year without increasing food intake would decrease body weight by 18 pounds in a year. In other words, if you walk at 4.0 mph for 45 minutes a day for a year, you'll lose 18 pounds, provided you don't increase your food intake.

Let's look at it another way. Suppose you're at the correct weight and want to use your fitness walking program to let you splurge a little. What can you eat with the extra 300 calories you burn in a fitness walking session? Here's a list of foods that contain about 300 calories:

One McDonald's cheeseburger
Two egg bagels
One cup of potato salad
One piece of lemon meringue pie

You could eat any of these *extra* foods over and above your regular diet if you fitness walked briskly for 54 minutes a day or up a moderate incline 25 minutes a day.

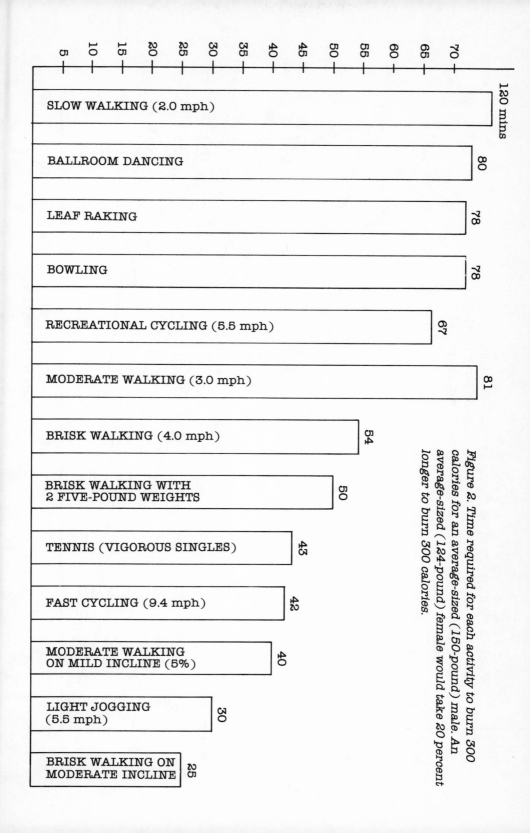

Figure 2. Time required for each activity to burn 300 calories for an average-sized (150-pound) male. An average-sized (124-pound) female would take 20 percent longer to burn 300 calories.

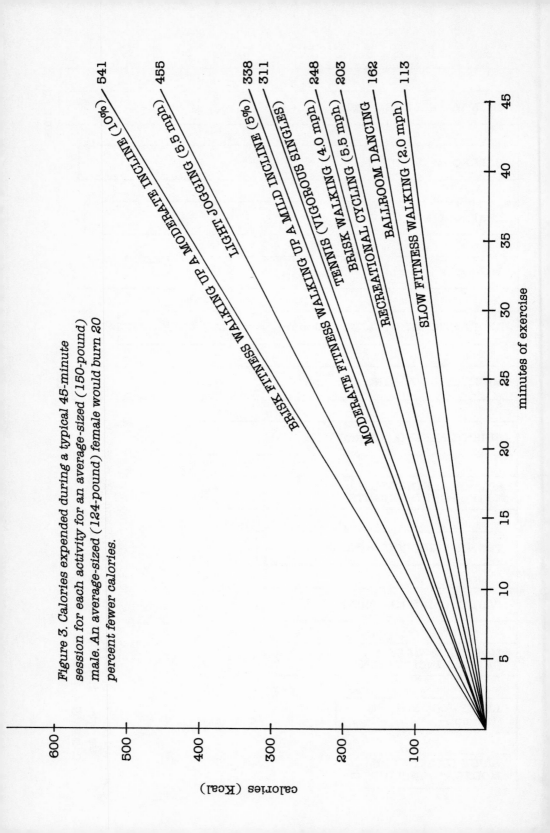

Figure 3. Calories expended during a typical 45-minute session for each activity for an average-sized (150-pound) male. An average-sized (124-pound) female would burn 20 percent fewer calories.

Let's look at this in still another way. Many people like to work out for a set amount of time each day. Forty-five minutes for a workout is a convenient amount of time for most people. Let's see how fitness walking compares with other activities when each is performed for 45 minutes. If you fitness walked briskly for 45 minutes, you would burn 248 calories, assuming you're average-sized. Add a mild, 5 percent incline and the calories rise to 338. Add 5 percent more incline and fitness walk for 45 minutes and the number of calories burned skyrockets to 541! Forty-five minutes of one of the advanced fitness walking programs will burn 100 more calories than light jogging (5.5 mph). Figure 3 summarizes how 45 minutes of fitness walking compares with other common activities.

Edward
Payson
Weston,
1839–1929.

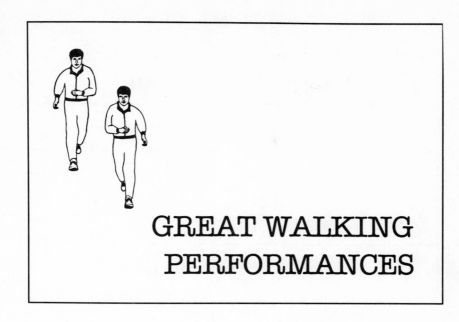

GREAT WALKING
PERFORMANCES

Rob Sweetgall is one of the great walkers of our time and his "50/50: A Walk for the Health of It" represents a monumental achievement. But there have been other great walkers throughout history. In fact, the sport of walking is not new to the United States at all. Before the turn of the century, walking contests were commonplace in America and walkers were some of the most celebrated athletes of the time.

Perhaps, Edward Payson Weston (1839–1929) is the most famous walker in American history. His walking contests regularly drew sellout crowds. In 1909, Weston walked from San Francisco to New York City in 104 days, averaging nearly 40 miles a day—at age seventy-one! Throughout his seventies he regularly outwalked men half his age. He lived to the ripe old age of ninety.

While Rob is young in his walking career, it's still fair to think of him as the inheritor of Weston's mantel as America's premier fitness walker. Just think of his achievement. We admire the achievements of individuals who compete in marathons, but compare that accomplishment to what Rob did in his 50/50 walk. By walking 11,600 miles in 363 days he averaged 32 miles a day. That's more than a marathon a day, every day for a year! All this through all kinds of weather, all alone.

end of 3 min = 136
3min exercise (30 sec) = 122

Fitness Walking Daily Log

DATE	WEEK	MILES WALKED
18.4	1	4.0 Km
21.4	1	4.5 Km
		WEEKLY MILEAGE =
		WEEKLY MILEAGE =
		WEEKLY MILEAGE =

WEATHER	COMMENTS (feelings, etc.)

Fitness Walking Daily Log

DATE	WEEK	MILES WALKED
		WEEKLY MILEAGE =
		WEEKLY MILEAGE =
		WEEKLY MILEAGE =

WEATHER	COMMENTS (feelings, etc.)

Fitness Walking Daily Log

DATE	WEEK	MILES WALKED
		WEEKLY MILEAGE =
		WEEKLY MILEAGE =
		WEEKLY MILEAGE =

WEATHER	COMMENTS (feelings, etc.)

Fitness Walking Daily Log

DATE	WEEK	MILES WALKED
		WEEKLY MILEAGE =
		WEEKLY MILEAGE =
		WEEKLY MILEAGE =

WEATHER	COMMENTS (feelings, etc.)

"I hope to be walking the rest of my life," Rob answers to a student at one of the 300 major assembly programs throughout his U.S. travels. Photo by *Marysville–Yuba City (California) Appeal Democrat.*

ABOUT THE AUTHORS

The Walker

Robert J. Sweetgall is the executive director and founder of the Foundation for the Development of Cardiovascular Health (FDCH), a public charity that organizes educational and research programs to improve awareness of lifestyle risk factors related to heart disease. Since creating the FDCH in 1981, Sweetgall has served as a peripatetic lecturer while trekking on two major journeys for a distance of 22,000 miles on foot in 21 months. In the process, he has spoken nationally on the subjects of health, aerobic fitness and walking to 125,000 students. Sweetgall is also an experienced ultramarathoner and has competed in four six-day races, each exceeding 300 miles. Sweetgall was born in Brooklyn, New York, in 1947, graduated with a chemical engineering degree from the Cooper Union in 1969 and worked for twelve years at the DuPont Company on a variety of engineering and consulting assignments. Motivated largely by four heart disease-related deaths in his own family within a single year, he retired from DuPont at age thirty-three to redirect his energies to wellness promotion. Volunteering his body as a human guinea pig for science, he now stands as the most extensively studied sports research subject in America and the only person in the world to have walked the equivalent of seven times across the North American continent in a span of three consecutive years.

The Doctor

Dr. James Rippe is a practicing cardiologist and medical director of the cardiac rehabilitation program at the University of Massachusetts, the largest such program in New England. He is also medical director of the university's Center for Health, Fitness and Human Performance. He is one of a new breed of doctors who have come to understand and believe in the beneficial effects of exercise on the heart. A lifelong and avid athlete himself, Dr. Rippe also holds a black belt in karate and, while attending Harvard Medical School, began a daily walk/jog regimen to maintain personal fitness. Because of the success of fitness walking for cardiac patients and his own personal commitment to exercise, Dr. Rippe is convinced that the medical profession ought to play a more active role in promoting exercise not just for heart patients but for all Americans.

The Exercise Scientist

Frank Katch, Ed.D., is chairman of the Department of Exercise Science at the University of Massachusetts at Amherst. Dr. Katch has written over 100 research articles in national and international research journals and three books on nutrition, weight control and exercise physiology. He has served as consultant on physical fitness and body composition to professional sport teams, including the New York Jets, Dallas Cowboys, Miami Dolphins and Boston Red Sox. He has studied male and female Olympic champions in track and field, canoe and kayak. He currently serves as a

Rob touched ground in all fifty states. This photo was taken on Day 144 in Hawaii, after 4,375 miles. Photo courtesy of AP Telephoto. ▶

trustee to the American College of Sports Medicine. He was particularly interested in how Rob Sweetgall's body adapted to the stress of walking more than 31 miles a day for 363 consecutive days. He designed the experiments to examine all aspects of Sweetgall's walk. For Katch, the scientific aspects of Sweetgall's performance allow a deeper look into themes that he has been exploring for many years. He has been a lifelong advocate of personal fitness and has made time for a daily walk or jog for the past sixteen years.